Changing Course, Changing Careers

By Mary Ann Bailey

WetFeet Insider Guide

WetFeet®

Helping you make smarter career decisions.

WetFeet, Inc.

The Folger Building
101 Howard Street
Suite 300
San Francisco, CA 94105

Phone: (415) 284-7900 or 1-800-926-4JOB
Fax: (415) 284-7910
Website: www.WetFeet.com

Changing Course, Changing Careers

By Mary Ann Bailey
ISBN: 1-58207-548-4

Table of Contents

Introduction

Whatever you can do or dream you can do, begin it.
Boldness has genius, power, and magic in it.
          —Goethe

Have you been thinking about changing careers? Maybe you have outgrown your current job and want to find something more challenging. Maybe you have been laid off and want a fresh start in a whole new career area. Or maybe you have reached a point in your professional life where you are ready to do something that is more congruent with your passions and values.

Whether you are thinking about changing careers out of desire or out of necessity, the prospect of initiating such a major life transition can be overwhelming. How do you decide what you want to do? Where do you get the information you need? How do you keep yourself motivated and on track so that you can reach your goals?

One minute you are imagining all the wonderful possibilities that are available to you, and the next minute you are immobilized by immense fear and doubt. You start to believe that changing careers may be a mistake—that you might be better off staying where you are. You begin to see that staying within your comfort zone, however draining and stressful it may be for you feels much safer and shields you from the fear and uncertainty that accompanies any change.

But changing careers does not have to be overwhelming. In fact, the process of changing careers can be one of the most exciting and self-affirming experiences you'll ever face. A transition gives you the time and space to reconnect with what's really important to you. It offers a wonderful opportunity to clarify what you want your next professional path to look like; and it gives you permission to pursue the dreams that have been dancing around the far corners of your mind.

I know how often people stop short of reaching their professional dreams. It is easy to get frustrated or impatient and give up, settling for your second, third, or even fourth job choice. But if you don't reach for your dream, you will never experience the joy of true professional satisfaction.

I have made several career changes in my own life, and I know how difficult this process can be. There have been times when I made a decision because it was easy, not because it was right. A job would fall into my lap, and I felt I it would be foolish and irresponsible not to take it. I ignored the little voice deep down in my gut telling me that if I just hung in there a little longer, the right job would appear. I let myself be swayed by the voices in my head, the critical voices that could hardly wait to let me know that I wasn't good enough, smart enough, or brave enough to get anything better than that job.

As a life coach who works with people going through career transitions, I hear similar stories everyday. People are being constantly torn between staying the course and finding a career path that feels good to them, or giving in to the pressure of uncertainty and fear and settling for "just a job." But I also see the rewards that people experience when they stay the course, follow their hearts, and reach their professional goals.

Changing careers is not just about finding a new job. It is about creating a new professional life—but this process does not happen overnight. There are steps to take, questions to address, and information to gather. As with all processes, if you follow all of the steps, you will most likely succeed. But if you attempt to bypass or eliminate some of the steps, you will definitely run into trouble.

The process of changing careers is also more successful when you enlist the help of other people. You need people who can help give you direction, point you toward information and resources, provide new insight and creative suggestions, cheer you on, and hold you accountable. And you need people who believe in you, so that you can learn to better believe in yourself. Changing careers is a multifaceted journey; and as with any journey, the better prepared you are, the more satisfying and successful the experience will be.

This book is intended as a guide for people who are ready to start this journey. I have broken down the process of changing careers into practical steps that are easy to understand and implement. I have included information, questions, and exercises that will help you evaluate your readiness to change careers, better understand the process of change, assess your skills and talents, and clarify your passions and values. I have also incorporated strategies, resources, and real people profiles that will assist you in creating your next professional path. Once you have decided on your path, the book will guide you through the development and implementation of a workable action plan to ensure you reach your goals.

INSIDER TIP

Changing careers is a journey; the better prepared you are, the more satisfying and direct the route to your destination will be.

This book includes several sets of exercises designed to support you, while others are meant to challenge you. Some exercises will help you work through the resistance, fear, and uncertainty that always seem to accompany any major change. Other exercises will encourage you to step outside your comfort zone, consider new ideas, and experiment with new ways of thinking and acting. Finally, I've also included some exercises that will engage your creativity and encourage you to stretch your boundaries.

Throughout the book, I have tried to balance information with inspiration, creativity with practicality, and action with thought. I know that each of us is motivated differently. Some of us are energized by an action-oriented focus, while others find their energy through inspiration and contemplation. With this book, I hope that every reader can find the motivation to keep moving toward a new professional path.

I hope that you find this book helpful as you begin the process of choosing a new career. I know that you are capable of designing the career of your dreams and living the life you want. It doesn't matter who you are or what your situation is. If you are determined, if you commit fully to the process, and if you believe in your ability to succeed, you will be successful.

Getting Your Bearings

Are You Ready?

Understanding Change

Assessing Your Readiness

Seven Core Life Skills

Your Next Move

You must begin wherever you are.
    —Jack Boland

When we think about making a change in our lives, most of us immediately think about the endpoint. What is it we want to achieve? Where do we want to end up? Knowing where we are heading is a crucial piece of the change process. How will we know that we've reached our goal if we are not sure where we are going?

But there is another important part of the process of change that is often overlooked: clearly defining your starting point. Where exactly are you in your life? Are you ready to make a change? What knowledge and skills are you starting with, and what kinds of information and competencies are you going to need to acquire along the way? Where do you see yourself getting stuck?

Failing to clearly define your starting point is a little like using a map to find your way to someplace you've never been, but failing to consider your point of origin. Knowing where you're headed is only half of the equation. To get there without making a lot of wrong turns, you'll also need to know where you're starting from. Only then can you determine the shortest, fastest, or safest route to your destination.

This chapter is about identifying your starting point: You'll assess your level of readiness to pursue a career change, you'll learn about the systemic process of change, and you'll have an opportunity to evaluate your personal comfort level with change. The last section provides an assessment tool to help you evaluate your competency levels in the seven skill areas required for making any kind of major personal change.

Are You Ready?

Are you really ready for a career change? That may sound like a silly question in a book about changing careers; but wanting to change careers and being ready to change careers are not always the same thing. Sometimes factors in our lives preclude an immediate change. It doesn't mean you will never be able to pursue a different career; it just means that if you try to make a change in the midst of too many other pressures, you probably won't be as successful as you would like.

It's important to take the time to carefully assess your overall readiness to embark on this journey, before making any final decisions. In assessing your readiness, you should consider five key areas.

REASONS FOR CHANGING CAREERS

First, let's look at why you're thinking about changing careers. When considering a career change, people are usually coming from one of two perspectives:

1. Some consider a career change in response to unpleasant work situation. Their primary goal is to escape the stress and anxiety they are experiencing at work. What their next career will be is a secondary concern.

2. Others consider a career change as a forward-looking decision. Although they, too, may be unhappy at work, they are looking ahead. They know there are other careers that will excite and challenge them, and they are ready to take the time to figure out what those careers may be.

The difference in these two scenarios is the kind of energy involved. When you are moving toward something, even if it's just the vaguest of ideas, you are working with positive energy. And the action of pursuing something new and exciting will maintain your energy and keep you motivated throughout the process. However, if your reason for changing careers is the desire to escape discomfort, you are using a more negative energy that will quickly evaporate as soon as you relieve that discomfort.

Which scenario best describes your situation? Are you running from or moving toward something? What kind of energy are you bringing to this change? You don't want to get halfway into this process and then realize that you really don't have the desire or momentum to see it through to completion.

CURRENT JOB STATUS

Now take some time to look at your present job status. Are you currently employed and fairly secure in your job? If so, this might be a good time to begin the process of changing careers. You have a steady income and you have job security, so there is no real external pressure to find a new job right away. Although you may be in a hurry to change careers, you know you have the resources and the time necessary to work through this transition process thoughtfully and deliberately. This is the ideal situation and will greatly enhance your probability of success.

But what if you are currently unemployed or will soon be unemployed? Being in this position does not necessarily mean that you aren't ready to make a change at this time, but it does raise some important questions. How financially secure are you? How long can you comfortably afford to be unemployed? Given your current job status, how emotionally ready are you to undertake this career change? Would it feel better to wait?

Depending on your answers to these questions, it might be useful to think about taking a transitional job. This job might be in a similar field and require skills you already have. It need not be the most exciting of jobs, but it should be sufficient to pay the bills and allow you a little more breathing space, so that you can start thinking more seriously about changing careers without the additional stress of financial or time constraints.

You are the only one who knows what causes you stress and anxiety, so you have to make the decision that is best for you and your family. However, it is important to remember that the process of changing careers is often stressful on its own; therefore, the fewer pressures and fears that you begin with, the smoother the journey.

FINANCIAL IMPACT

As is clear from the previous section, financial issues play a key role in determining whether you are ready to embark on a career change. So, it is imperative that you take the time to carefully assess the cost of making this kind of change and the impact it will have, both financially and emotionally, on you and your family.

First, look at the bottom line. How much will this transition cost? Although it can be difficult to determine the exact cost of a career transition, it is better to overestimate rather than underestimate the expenses involved. A good rule of thumb is to have enough money to cover your living expenses for at least 6 months. One of the biggest stressors that people face during a career transition is not having enough money to comfortably see them through the process.

Even if you are planning on staying in your current job as you search for a new one, it is wise to have that extra money set aside in case something unexpected happens. You might decide it would be more expedient to leave your job and work on your career change full time. Or, you might unexpectedly lose your job in the middle of the transition. If you have planned ahead and have put money aside, you will be able to continue your search without the extra stress and anxiety of financial worries.

If you are planning to start your own business, you will need savings to cover 6 months of living expense in addition to the start-up costs of your particular business. Start-up costs can be steep, and it is important to do the research up front to get an accurate sense of just how much it will cost to get your business up and running. Very few businesses are profitable from the beginning, so having a strong financial foundation from the start can make the difference between succeeding and failing.

Also, if you are thinking about going back to school, it is important to know the cost of the specific program and have a clear plan for paying for it. Will you get a loan? If so, what steps do you need to take to make that happen? How will the cost of the loan affect your financial situation and how do you plan to pay off the loan?

You must also consider how great a financial and emotional sacrifice you are willing to make to change careers. What if, for some unforeseen reason, you can't find the job you want in the time you have allotted? If you are the only person you are responsible for, it might be okay to sacrifice some of the elements of comfort during this time to save money. However, if you have a partner, or particularly, if you have children, they may not be as content making the same kind of sacrifices. How will you know when the transition has become too expensive?

You may be tempted to ignore these questions and just hope for the best. But that has proved to be a very poor strategy. It is much more effective to address these issues up front with all those involved. Take the time to develop a financial plan for your transition. Having a document that accurately outlines your expenses will help you look more objectively at the viability of changing careers at this time. Then create a timeline that clearly indicates how much time you are willing to dedicate to this process and how much money you can afford to spend.

And remember, a career change affects everyone in your home, so it is important that everyone is aware of what is happening and has some input into your transition plan. Everyone has their own fears, beliefs, and judgments around money and having these kinds of discussions can be difficult. But taking the time to talk about the issues and bringing the fears and concerns out in the open before the process starts will alleviate a great deal of anxiety, conflict, and misunderstanding down the road.

IMPACT ON YOUR FAMILY

The next issue is how this change will affect your family. The process of designing a new career path is time-consuming. You may not be as available as you have been, and your spouse or partner may need to assume more responsibilities around the house. Will this be okay with your spouse or partner?

How does your career change fit into your family's long-range plan? Have you created a timeline and financial strategy that ensure that your career change will not undermine your spouse's, partner's, or children's goals?

Is it possible that your new career will require your family to move? Moving can be an emotional subject, especially if you have children or have relatives close by.

Is your spouse or partner comfortable with the financial plan you've made? If there are financial sacrifices that will have to be made, is your spouse on board? Will he or she have to go back to work? Is that okay?

It may be that changing professions will be the best thing in the world for you and your family. You may have a career in mind that would be less stressful for you, that would allow you to spend more time at home, and that would provide financial security. Only after laying out all the facts, addressing everyone's concerns, and honestly assessing the overall impact of your decision, will you be able to truthfully determine whether this is a good time for you to make this move.

PERSONAL COMMITMENT

The last issue to examine is your level of commitment to making this transition. Making any kind of life change is difficult because changes elicit resistance, and the bigger the change, the greater the resistance. Changing careers is a major life transition, so you can expect to run into a lot of resistance along the way, both external and internal.

If you are fully committed to making this change, you will be able to draw on the power of your commitment to help you push through the resistance as it comes up. But if you are only lukewarm to the idea of changing careers, you are not likely to have the strength to successfully confront the obstacles and hurdles that lie before you.

Commitment is a word that is overused and whose meaning has been diluted over the years. It can be easy to think that you are committed to something when it would be more accurate to say that you want to make a change or that you think you should make a change. Simply wanting or thinking you should change careers is not the same as knowing in your heart of hearts that you can find a career that is more exciting and fulfilling and that you are willing to do what it takes to make it happen.

Only you can know how committed you are to the process of changing careers now. So, be honest with yourself. How committed are you? How badly do you want this? If you find that the prospect of changing careers does not hold enough energy for you right now, let it go. You would be doing yourself, and your family, a great disservice to embark on this journey on only a half tank of commitment.

But if you know deep in your heart that this is the right thing to do, and if you are ready and willing to devote the time and energy needed to make this change, then go for it. Your journey will still have its share of ups and downs; but the power of your commitment and desire to make this change will help you overcome any obstacles.

Understanding Change

We live in a world of ever-present change. We experience near-constant change in all areas of our personal and professional lives. You might think that with all this practice we would be fairly adept at making changes. But the fact of the matter is that making any kind of life change, whether large or small, can still be difficult.

Some of the difficulty lies in the very nature of change. All systems resist change and will do what they can to maintain the status quo. Other problems can arise because of our own level of comfort with change. Much of the difficulty arises because we don't know what to expect. We are sometimes blindsided by unforeseen obstacles. It is easy to become frustrated and think we are doing something wrong, when much of the time, what we are experiencing is just a normal part of the change process. Becoming more familiar with the different aspects of change is the key to avoiding these common pitfalls.

How would you describe your comfort with change? Does change make you anxious? Do you get excited thinking about the possibilities that change offers? Or are you not really clear about feelings? A simple way to find out how you relate to change is to do the following exercise:

Take something that you do on a regular basis and make a change in your routine. For example, if you always listen to a classical music station, change and listen to a rock station. If you always take the same route in your morning run, find a new route. If you like to watch reality TV, watch some shows on the Discovery Channel or PBS. It doesn't matter what the change is, just that it is something different from your normal pattern.

As you think about making the change, pay attention to the kinds of thoughts and feelings you have about the change. Do you feel energized? Do you feel resistant? Do you think this is dumb?

Then make the change. What do you notice? What are you thinking and feeling now? What insights did you have? Maybe you found out that change is not as scary as you thought. Maybe you saw how changing one small thing can broaden your perspective. Or maybe you realized that stepping outside your comfort zone and changing a routine made you nervous.

The point here isn't really whether you are afraid of change. The point is becoming aware of how you react to change so that you will be better able to recognize the obstacles before they become problems.

STUCK IN HOMEOSTASIS

All systems resist change, and human beings are no exception. When we are disturbed by something trying to alter our state of being, an internal mechanism kicks in to return us to a state of equilibrium. This process is known as *homeostasis*. Homeostasis is the ability of an organism to maintain internal equilibrium by making physiological adjustments.

So, when people say they are not comfortable with change, some of that discomfort probably has a biological root. I won't go into great scientific detail here, but I think it can be very useful to understand the connection between the resistance and fear we can experience with change and the physiology of the human brain.

Human brains have three main parts: The brain stem is the part of the brain that wakes us up, puts us to sleep, and reminds our hearts to beat. The midbrain regulates our body temperature, houses our emotions, and governs our fight-or-flight response that keeps us alive in the face of danger. The cortex is the part that makes us human: Art, music, and science all live here, along with our rational thoughts and creative impulses.

Separately, these parts of the brain all work well. It is the interaction of the parts that sometimes can cause us problems, especially when it comes to making changes in our lives. When the midbrain senses a threat, it goes into its fight-or-flight mode. Our heart starts to beat faster, our palms get sweaty, and our breathing becomes more rapid. We are being alerted to the need to take action. This is good because is can protect us from danger.

But another part of the fight-or-flight response is a slowing or cessation of cortical functions (dictated by the cortex, the rational part of the brain), because the midbrain doesn't want us to stop and take time to creatively ponder the situation when we need to be fleeing from a burning building, for example. And this is why we sometimes feel creatively blocked when we want to make a change in our lives.

When the midbrain senses something new or unfamiliar, it may perceive it as a potential threat. When this happens, the midbrain reacts predictably, shutting or slowing down our creative and rational thinking abilities. As a result, we feel stuck, frozen, or overwhelmed and have a difficult time following through with our change. In order to move forward and achieve our goal, we need to find a way to bypass this fight-or-flight response of our midbrain.

BABY STEPS

One way to sidestep the fight-or-flight response is to set a series of goals that are each minor enough to go undetected by the fear center of the brain. When we try to do too much or make too drastic a change all at once, our fear center is alerted to the perceived threat. If the fear center is not disturbed, however, our cortex, or creative brain, will be free to play its part, uninterrupted by the midbrain.

This is important because our cortex is where the brain develops new mental "software" and pathways to facilitate new behaviors. Because they are not perceived as threats, small steps provide the creative freedom and stability we need to make necessary behavioral changes deliberately and thoughtfully. This gradual assimilation results in long-lasting change.

Understanding how your mind and body react to the threat of change can help you plan your strategy accordingly. If you have a low level of comfort with change, then you know that you will need to take smaller steps. If you are less susceptible to fear, you will probably be able to move more quickly. It also can be reassuring to understand that the fear and resistance you may experience is the result of a normal physiological process, as opposed to a personal failing or shortcoming.

Assessing Your Readiness

The process of changing careers will require you to draw on an array of personal skills and competencies. You will need to make decisions, take risks, think creatively, be resilient, and believe in your ability to meet the challenges. At times you will need to examine your thinking and behavior to determine whether they are sabotaging the process; at times, you will need to turn to your support system for strength.

How would you assess your life skills? What are your strengths and weaknesses? Too often we don't take the time at the beginning of a transition to accurately assess our competencies. Thus, we become aware of our skill gaps only after we fall into them.

The "Core Skill Assessment" exercise offers a quick and easy way to determine your competence and comfort with seven life skills that will be tested repeatedly during the course of your career change—indeed, they are an integral part of any life change. This is not a test. The purpose of the assessment is to get a definitive picture of where you are right now. This information will enable you to be more proactive in planning your strategy.

CORE SKILL ASSESSMENT

Read each statement carefully and rate yourself as honestly as possible, circling the number that corresponds to the frequency with which you practice each skill. Try not to over- or underestimate your abilities. Think about times when you needed to use these skills. When did you feel successful? Review the times that didn't go as well. Can you remember what happened, where you got stuck? The more examples you can remember, the more accurate your assessment will be.

	Never	Rarely	Sometimes	Often	Always
1. I make decisions easily.	1	2	3	4	5
2. I am comfortable taking risks.	1	2	3	4	5
3. I enjoy thinking creatively to solve a problem.	1	2	3	4	5
4. I am resilient; I don't let obstacles stop me.	1	2	3	4	5
5. I am willing to consider how my thoughts and behaviors might be sabotaging my progress.	1	2	3	4	5
6. I have a good support system.	1	2	3	4	5
7. I believe I can achieve any goal I set for myself.	1	2	3	4	5

As you may have noticed, there is no place for your total score, and there aren't scoring categories such as excellent, good, or fair. There is no rating system because you are the only person who can accurately evaluate your level of skill in each of these areas. You know which areas cause more difficulty for you, and that is the purpose of this exercise: to identify potential problem areas that may surface during your career transition.

If you have given yourself all 4s and 5s, you are feeling very competent in these areas and ready to start the process of changing careers. If you have circled more 1s and 2s, you may want to seriously consider putting off pursuing a career change until you have had a chance to improve some of these skills. You will need to draw on all of these skills for a career change, and if you are starting with a deficit in several areas, you will very likely experience more obstacles and missteps than necessary.

Seven Core Life Skills

Even those who selected all 4s and 5s will find themselves challenged by the process of changing careers and will need to be prepared for those challenges. The seven skills described in this section will be tested for anyone who pursues a career change. It will help to understand in advance the role of each skill in the change process. For each, I also offer suggestions to help you increase your competence and confidence so that you will be able to navigate your career change with as little stormy weather as possible.

DECISION MAKING

Making decisions is a fundamental life skill. The fact that you are reading this book indicates that you are pursuing a decision regarding your career path. If you make the decision to change careers, you will then be faced with many other decisions: How will you go about the process? What path will you pursue? What kinds of job offers will interest you?

Being comfortable with how you make decisions is a crucial part of embracing the process of change. There is no one correct way to make decisions. Each of us has our own style. The key, however, is to be very aware of what that style is so that we can begin to recognize those patterns of our behavior that are helpful and those that create stumbling blocks.

How do you make decisions? Are you someone who makes decisions quickly, or are you more methodical? Do you need to gather lots of information, or are you satisfied with a smaller set of relevant facts? Do you seek input from other people, or do you prefer to figure things out on your own?

Decision making is not an exact science. The outcome is not guaranteed no matter how carefully you think about your decision—and therein lies the rub. You will always be presented with several choices; how will you know which choice is the right one for you?

Some people deal with these feelings of uncertainty by making decisions quickly and ignoring or denying the emotional aspect of their decisions. Others find themselves frozen by the weight of their decision and the impact it could have on all involved. Neither of these methods is particularly effective. When you find yourself in this situation, it helps to have a process in place that can assist you in refocusing on the issue at hand.

Following are some questions designed to provide that structure. The next time you find yourself getting stuck when you need to make a decision, take some time to answer these questions. Your answers could provide the jumpstart you need to get the decision-making process moving forward again.

1. What is the actual decision I need to make? What is the core issue? What is the objective of this decision?

2. Can I break this decision down into smaller parts? Is there more than one issue involved? How can I separate them out so that I have a clearer picture of my goals?

3. How many people and how much information do I really need to make this decision? (Too much input can be as detrimental as too little.)

4. What is my gut telling me? (Once you get all the information you need, it may be useful to sit calmly by yourself and listen to what your body and heart are telling you.)

5. Where can I get the support I need when I am feeling stuck, scared, or unsure of how to proceed? (Make sure you have one or two people who will be willing to support you in this process. These should be people who will be willing to listen and ask the kinds of questions that will help you clarify your decision.)

And finally, once you have made your decision, go with it. Don't spend time second-guessing yourself. Have confidence in your decision, knowing that you approached it thoughtfully. Then look forward to the opportunities afforded you by this decision.

RISK TAKING

Any major change involves some risk, because change requires you to leave something familiar behind and move toward something new and unfamiliar. Changing careers is a big adjustment that comes with its own set of risks.

The first and most obvious risk is that of failure. What if you don't achieve your goals? What will happen? Then there is the risk of being disappointed when you do reach your goal because it is not what you had expected. There may be a financial risk. And there is the risk that you will change your mind halfway through, having already dedicated a great deal of time and energy to the change.

There is also the risk of trusting the little voice inside you that is telling you to go for it when everyone is saying you're nuts. And there is the risk of alienating those who don't want you to make this change, whether because they fear that your relationship will change or because it causes them to question how they are living their lives.

Then there is the biggest risk of all—the risk that you will be successful. You are taking the risk that your life will really change and that you will be able to step into your dream.

As strange as it sounds, being successful can be a little frightening. You may not have had many opportunities to pursue and realize your personal goals. You may wonder whether achieving those goals will be as satisfying as you have hoped. You may feel that you don't deserve to be successful. But don't let those feelings get in the way of experiencing all the joy, excitement, and personal fulfillment that come from reaching your goal and living your dream.

How comfortable are you with taking risks? Some people are excited by this kind of adventure. Others respond with anxiety and fear. It is important to know where you fall on this continuum so that you can take the steps necessary to care for yourself and alleviate your discomfort before it sabotages your career change.

It is certainly possible to expand your comfort with risk taking. The first step is to increase your awareness of what exactly is making you uncomfortable, so you can then take steps to lessen or eliminate that fear. The "Taking Risks" exercise will help you begin that process.

RESILIENCE

No matter how carefully you map out your path to change, you will undoubtedly experience your share of obstacles and pitfalls. That is the very nature of change. What is important is not whether you trip over an obstacle, but how you recover from the fall.

There are several possible reactions when something does not go as planned. You could blame yourself for something you did or did not do. Or you could blame someone else. Neither reaction is particularly constructive because each one shifts your focus away from your goal.

Another possible reaction is to use the misstep as a learning experience. Mistakes can provide all sorts of useful information if you are open to learning from them. You may learn something about the effectiveness of your strategy, the assumptions you are making, the beliefs you are holding on to, or the communication style you're using. This is all valuable insight because it gives you the data you need to course-correct.

So, when you do encounter a setback (and you will), just remember that it is much easier to bounce back when you separate yourself from the incident. If you get caught up in the nitty-gritty of what went wrong and who's to blame, you will just get bogged down. But if you can keep your eyes on the prize and keep working toward your goals, you will be amazed at how resilient you can be.

TAKING RISKS

Using the questions below, observe yourself as you go through your day. Answer these questions as if you are a scientist gathering data, objectively and without judgment. Be as open and honest as possible. Make notes so that you can begin to see patterns.

1. What risk(s) did you take today?

_____

_____

_____

2. What facilitated your taking the risk?

_____

_____

_____

3. What was the outcome?

_____

_____

_____

4. What risk(s) did you avoid taking?

_____

_____

_____

TAKING RISKS (CONT'D)

5. What impeded you from taking the risk?

_____

_____

_____

6. What were the consequences, if any, of not taking the risk?

_____

_____

_____

7. What patterns do you see in your approach to risk taking?

_____

_____

_____

8. What actions will you take based on your observations?

_____

_____

_____

SELF-MOTIVATION

Have you ever noticed that, at the beginning of a project, you have a lot of energy and enthusiasm, but then, as the project moves forward, the pace slows and you begin to lose focus? Maybe you avoid or put off completing some of the less appealing tasks. Maybe you begin to second-guess yourself. Or maybe you find yourself giving in to self-doubt. If you have experienced any of these feelings, you have come face to face with the effects of sabotaging behaviors.

Sabotaging behaviors are thought patterns and actions you have adopted over the years that prevent you from reaching your goals. There are many kinds of sabotaging behaviors, including procrastination, self-doubt, taking on more than you can reasonably handle, setting unrealistic goals, and holding on to outdated beliefs. Often they are difficult to identify because they are so deeply ingrained in your everyday thoughts and actions. They have become reflexive behaviors and, as such, feel perfectly normal—in fact, you may not be aware of them at all. Like bad posture, nail-biting, or using "um" to punctuate your conversations, they're bad habits you repeat with such frequency that you often fail to register their occurrence at all. And all they do is hamper your progress.

The best way to avoid becoming ensnared by these patterns is to become very aware of your particular patterns. Which habits are helping you and which are hindering your success? Once you recognize your bad habits, you will be able to take steps to eliminate them.

Maybe you are nagged by the voice of self-doubt. If so, try giving yourself a pep talk instead. Practice encouraging yourself. Maybe you sabotage yourself with unreasonably high expectations and then prove your incompetence by failing to meet them. If that's the case, try lowering your expectations a bit to see what happens. If you are prone to procrastination, resolve to attack unpleasant tasks (or whichever tasks you tend to avoid) first or to alternate your least-favorite tasks with those you aren't tempted to procrastinate.

The key is to become aware of the actions and thought patterns that are barriers to your success. Once you identify how you are sabotaging yourself, you will be able to trade in those behaviors for ones that will facilitate your progress.

MAINTAINING A SUPPORT SYSTEM

Support systems are a crucial, but often overlooked, element of successful life changes. Given the inevitable risks, mistakes, and obstacles that accompany any major transition, you will absolutely need a network of people you can turn to for resources, support, and validation when needed.

You may not be comfortable asking for help or support. Our culture emphasizes independence and self-sufficiency. But trying to make this kind of change by yourself will be much harder. Consider any successful person you admire, whether in business, sports, or the arts, and you'll see that most have support teams making sure their needs are met and resources are available. In fact, many times, the most successful people work with the support of extensive professional and personal support teams. In most professions, the higher you go up the ladder, the greater the support system at your disposal. That's no mistake; it's most definitely by design.

See "Assembling a Support System" in the next chapter for advice on asking for and accepting help and specific steps for putting together a support network that will best serve your needs.

BELIEVING IN YOURSELF

Believing that you can achieve your goals is the most important of the seven core skills.

The path of change is often bumpy. There will be times when you face obstacles and will be tempted to give up. There will be times when you will wonder what on earth you are doing. And there will be times when the light at the end of the tunnel will flicker out of view and you will seriously think about turning back. But, if you honestly believe you can reach your goal, you will likely reach it.

Believing in yourself does not mean you will not have moments of doubt. It means that when you do encounter a setback or find your motivation waning, you will be able to draw on your core belief in yourself to pull you out of the slump and begin moving forward again.

But believing in yourself is not always easy, because some experiences in life challenge that belief. You may have accumulated a lot of negative messages during your lifetime, many of which you have come to believe are true. Perhaps you have experienced failures and now hold those as evidence that you are likely to fail again. There may even be others who question your ability to succeed.

LIKE RIDING A BIKE?

Remember, no one ever learned to ride a bike by looking behind them. Maintain your focus on where you are headed, not where you have been or where you are.

All this doubt can easily destabilize you, and when you feel unmoored or off center, you will begin to question whether you can succeed. So, throughout this transition, whenever you begin to doubt your decisions, abilities, or goals, take some time to yourself—whether you choose to sit quietly or go for a run—and reconnect with why you are making this change. Remind yourself of all the thought and planning you put into the decision. Tap back into your excitement, your creativity, and your strongly held belief that there is something bigger and better waiting for you. Refocus your sights on the bigger picture and you will return to your center—and you will believe in your ability to succeed.

PUTTING IT ALL TOGETHER

At this point, I invite you to go back and repeat the "Core Skill Assessment" to see how your assessment of your skills has changed after reading about each of the core skills. We all have a tendency to initially over- or underrate ourselves because we are looking at the questions through our narrow window on the world. But now that you have more information, your view may have expanded, allowing you to more accurately assess your skills and competencies. And as I have stressed, the greater your awareness of your strengths and gaps, the better your ability to develop successful strategies for achieving your goals.

Before moving on to the end of this chapter, take some time to review what you have read so far about change, your relationship to change, and your overall readiness to jump into a career change. What thoughts are you having? How do you feel physically when you think about pursuing a new professional path? Taking all this into account will enable you to confidently decide what your next step will be.

Your Next Move

Are you ready to launch a career change? If your answer is yes, I applaud your decision. It takes great courage to step out of the ordinary and go for the extraordinary. Imagine what it would feel like to be working at a job that you love, that challenges you, and that you find satisfying and fulfilling. The journey you are about to embark on will give you the opportunity to create that kind of work—and life—for yourself.

But what if you are not ready to change careers at this time? What is your next step? Your next step will depend on your reasons for deciding not to make a career change at this time. If you have come to realize that you don't have the full commitment, desire, or need to pursue a new professional path right now, then it would probably be best to shelve this idea for a while. But make sure you revisit it periodically. When the time is right for you to make the change, you will know it.

If you have decided against pursuing a career change right now because of certain obstacles, then your next move could be to take steps to remove these obstacles. If money is the issue, you could prepare a financial plan that would enable you to save the money you need to go back to school or to support yourself between jobs. If your life is overbooked, you might look at how to divest yourself of extra commitments so that you will have the time and energy needed to focus on this process. Or if you have come to realize that your life skills are not as strong as you will need to make such a change, you may want to work with a mentor or coach to help you develop your competencies so that you will be better prepared when you do decide to make a change. You could also turn to a trusted friend or family member to help you.

Taking specific steps to remove the obstacles between you and your goal is empowering. You will no longer feel stuck or trapped. Even if it takes some time to clear your path, you will know that you are working toward something that is important to you. As the obstacles are removed, possibilities will open up for you, and you will be on your way to creating and living a satisfying life.

This chapter was about getting your bearings and assessing your readiness to make a career change. Only you know whether this is the right time for you to initiate such a change. If you know there are issues you need to address before you can start, then it's important to take the time necessary to resolve them. The more prepared you are to make a change, the more successful the process will be.

But if you're ready to take the leap and change your career, then let's get started!

Planning Your Route

Assembling a Support System

Assessing Your Skills and Talents

Clarifying Your Values, Passions, and Interests

Defining Your Ideal Work Environment

Identifying Your Dream Job

Developing an Action Plan

Before anything else, preparation is the key to success.
—Alexander Graham Bell

You are about to embark on the exciting adventure of discovering your next career path. And as with any adventure, the better your preparations, the better the trip. In this chapter, you will make sure you have all the necessary pieces in place to ensure your success when you take your first step toward implementing your action plan.

Each section in this chapter represents an important piece of preparation for this journey; it is important to take the time to read each section carefully and complete all the exercises. I recommend that you buy a notebook or journal to record all the information you gather from the exercises. Much like preparing for a long trip to an exotic land, you'll need to make some notes about things you have to do before you leave to ensure a hassle-free trip.

At times you may feel impatient and want to jump ahead, or you may feel that you know all this stuff and don't want or need to complete all of the exercises. These are common feelings and are usually telltale signs that your system is sensing an impending change.

If you do get the urge to skip ahead, the best thing to do is to take a break and engage in some sort of physical activity such as a walk, yoga, or a short run. Physical exercise will clear your mind, dissipate any nervous energy, and help you regain your focus.

You are taking a significant step, and it makes sense to make sure that you take all the time and thought you need to prepare for it. Besides, planning a trip you've dreamed about for a long time is part of the fun.

Assembling a Support System

Having a strong and reliable support system support is critical for any major transition. Who will you call when you are feeling stuck, discouraged, or like giving up? Who will you celebrate with when you are successful? Who will be there to prod you, encourage you, and remind you how great you are and that what you are doing is exciting and courageous? And who will you turn to when you need information, resources, or a new perspective?

Developing this kind of safety net enables you to share the burden of your career change with others and lighten your load. It also helps ensure success, as a team effort is usually more successful than a solo performance. But many resist putting a support system into place. You may be uncomfortable asking for help. It can also be a little scary to publicize your dreams. Once you tell others what you are planning to do, they will be watching you, asking about your progress, and witnessing your missteps. What if you fall short? What if you fall flat on our face? What will they think?

There is always a chance that the people in your support network will have some critical opinions about what you do or don't do. But it has been my experience that most of us are our own worst critic—having a group of people behind us who believe in us and what we are doing is a great way to alleviate many of our fears and concerns.

So, how do you create a support system that will be most beneficial to you? It is important to choose your supporters carefully and to accept that not everyone will be supportive of change in others. When you decide to make a change in your life, you cause small ripples of change in the lives of those around you.

The effects may be as direct as not being as available to your friends as you once were, or they may be indirect, such as a shift in your values or philosophy of life. These shifts can be threatening: Your friends may begin to wonder, "Am I really happy in my job?"

or think, "I really want to change jobs, too, but I'm not sure I have the nerve." These questions and concerns may make it difficult to be as supportive as they could be. They may be threatened, however subtly, by the change you are pursuing.

So, it is sometimes necessary to go outside your group of friends and family to find the support you need. Some places to find extra support include workshops, seminars, or classes where you could meet people going through a similar process. Career counselors and coaches can provide objectivity, accountability, and resources. And there are many businesses and organizations that provide information and services to people who are changing careers. Support is available. It is just a matter of developing a support system that will best serve your individual needs.

The "Building Support" exercise will help you identify your support needs and people and resources you can turn to when you are in need of the kindness of others.

As you go through the exercise, pay attention to the feelings and thoughts you have. Asking for help can be difficult for many reasons, and it's important to anticipate where you could run into trouble. Perhaps you believe that asking for help is a sign of weakness. Maybe you feel that you are bothering people when you ask for help. Or maybe you don't really believe you deserve anyone's help.

Examine whatever beliefs kick up for you. Do you really believe what you are telling yourself? If someone came to you and asked for your help, would you think them to be weak or bothersome? Probably not, so see if you can give yourself the same compassion that you show your friends.

Changing careers is a complex process, and there is no shame in seeking strength in numbers. Realize that it is not a weakness to draw on the resources, talents, knowledge, and support of others. Being able to anticipate obstacles and planning to overcome them with the help of others is not a sign of weakness. It's a sign of commitment and resolve.

BUILDING SUPPORT

1. Make a list below of all the areas in which you will want or need support as you pursue your career change. Examples: emotional support, accountability, finding information and resources, a sounding board or devil's advocate, creative thinking.

2. For each, ask yourself, "Who would be the best person to help me with this?" If you have someone in mind, write their name in the space provided; if not, leave it blank.

3. For needs you could not identify anyone to support you, ask yourself two questions: "Who do I know who might know someone who could help me with this?" "Where might I look to find help with this area?"

Support Need   **Best Person/Resource**

_____   _____

_____   _____

_____   _____

_____   _____

_____   _____

_____   _____

_____   _____

4. Now that you have your list of supporters and resources, think about exactly what you will ask each of them to do, specifically how you want them to help you, and how you might sabotage the process.

5. When you are clear about what you want of your team members, meet with each to ask whether they are willing and able to help and support you. Establishing guidelines and expectations will make it much easier for you to ask for help and for them to respond. Taking the time to talk to them in advance will demonstrate not only your respect for their skills and time but also your commitment to this process.

Assessing Your Skills and Talents

A common barrier to finding truly fulfilling work is the inability to clearly articulate the skills you have, the skills you want to use, and the skills you want to strengthen or develop. Before you can choose a career path that will be both professionally challenging and personally rewarding, you must identify and prioritize your skills, talents, and interests, as well as name specific areas of knowledge and skills that you want to develop.

It can be very easy to take a job or follow a career path simply because it feels comfortable and familiar to you. You may opt to accept a job because it requires skills you know you have, even though you no longer enjoy using these particular skills. But somehow you allow yourself to get lulled into the comfort of the known, and, before long, you are bored, then frustrated, and eventually burned out.

You can take steps, however, to avoid this trap. You can complete a personal and professional skills inventory and a personal talents inventory. You can identify the knowledge and competencies you want to develop, and you can talk to friends and colleagues to get their perspective and input.

The point of the exercises in this section is to collect as much data as possible so that the decisions you make regarding your future career draw on all the experience and self-knowledge you have accumulated up to this point. Having a clear focus will enable you to be proactive, thus avoiding the common trap of reactively taking the road you've already been down before.

So, let's get started, shall we?

SKILLS

You can begin by using the "Skill Inventory" exercise to develop a complete list of the skills you have acquired throughout your life. As you work on this exercise, consider the Merriam-Webster definition of *skill*: "a learned power of doing something competently: a developed aptitude or ability." In other words, don't include innate abilities, or talents, in this list. This should be a list of *learned* abilities.

To ensure that you don't neglect to include skills you no longer use or skills that are now so second nature to you that you scarcely think of them as skills, I recommend that you start by considering each of your past jobs (start with your very first job, even an after-school job) and the specific skills you learned or honed in each. You may find it useful to refer to a copy of your resume, though you shouldn't limit yourself to skills highlighted on your resume. The point of this exercise is to prepare an exhaustive list of skills, regardless of whether you think each is relevant to your future career. Typical office skills include leadership, project management, organization, technical, teamwork, communication, and presentation skills.

Then move on to any volunteer or community activities you have participated in. Often we use different skills in our volunteer work than in our professional work. Examples of such skills are fundraising, managing volunteers, coaching, and community organizing.

Finally move to your personal life. Skills in this area may include relationship building, listening, and budgeting. Consider also skills from your hobbies and interests such as woodworking, gardening, or music.

Once the list is complete, star your top five skills—the skills that you enjoy and want to continue using. Then cross out the five skills that you no longer have any interest in using. For example, you may have developed strong mediation skills that you no longer want to use in your work.

SKILL INVENTORY

To be effective, this inventory should be all-inclusive, so take the time necessary to pre-pare a complete list. You need not finish this exercise in a single sitting. Coming back to it after you've had a chance to consider skills you'd forgotten about may be just what's needed.

Job skills:

_____

_____

_____

_____

_____

_____

_____

Volunteer or community skills:

_____

_____

_____

_____

_____

_____

_____

📄 SKILL INVENTORY (CONT'D)

Personal skills:

_____

_____

_____

_____

_____

_____

_____

TALENTS

Like the "Skill Inventory," the point of the "Talent Inventory" exercise is to prepare an exhaustive list of your talents. Talents are different from skills. Skills are learned, whereas talents are innate. When thinking about whether an ability is a skill or a talent, consider whether it's an ability you had to work on to develop or whether you seemed to know intuitively what was needed. What is a skill for one person may be a talent for another; for example, some have worked very hard to develop communication skills while others have a born knack for effective communication.

Each of us has our own set of talents, which might include specific academic abilities, artistic abilities, problem solving, reasoning, and interpersonal abilities. Understanding what your talents are and being comfortable acknowledging them will significantly increase your probability of finding a satisfying career that will challenge you and offer you a chance to grow and develop professionally.

Star your top three talents and cross out any talents you don't want to use in your work. For example, perhaps because of your talent for interpersonal interactions you have recently found yourself assuming the role of team leader. Maybe this isn't a role you enjoy, but a role you end up assuming simply because you are qualified to do so.

Focusing on our talents is not something that most of us spend much time doing. We either take them for granted or we downplay them because it seems self-aggrandizing to tout an ability we haven't worked to develop, but have come by naturally. But this is your chance to spend some time getting reacquainted with your innate talents.

TALENT INVENTORY

Personal talents:

_____

_____

_____

_____

_____

_____

_____

_____

DEVELOPMENT AREAS

Unlike the skill and talent exercises, the point of the "Development Area Inventory" is is identify only the skills and talents you want to further develop and use in your work.

Review your "Skill Inventory." Which skills have you wanted to further develop? Maybe you want to enhance your communication skills. Maybe you want to get more training in finance or management. Or maybe you realize you want to get more training in emotional intelligence work. Or maybe there are skills you've not yet had an opportunity to develop that you've always admired and wanted to pursue.

Then take a look at your "Talent Inventory." Is there anything on that list that you want to build on, any talents you've not been able to use as much as you'd like in your work? Would you like an opportunity to use your writing talent, your knack for problem solving, or your native technical aptitude?

As you develop this list, keep in mind that these should be skills and talents you personally and sincerely want to do, not things you think you should be doing to get ahead. The purpose of this exercise is to help you get a very clear picture of who you are and the gifts, skills, and talents you bring to the world. As you think about different career paths, you should be looking for something that fits who you are, not trying to adapt yourself to the job requirements.

DEVELOPMENT AREA INVENTORY

Top three skills:

_____

_____

_____

Top three talents:

_____

_____

_____

EXTERNAL INPUT

The last step in this process is to get some objective feedback on each of your skills, talents, and development areas. Although you probably have a pretty good sense of what you have to offer, chances are your perspective is fairly narrow and your assessment of your abilities is understated. So, to broaden your perspective, choose four or five of your friends or colleagues and ask them to give you their input. Make sure that the people you choose represent a good cross section of your life and that they will be open and honest with you.

Let them know that you are in the process of figuring out what kind of work you want to do and that you are trying to gather as much information about yourself as possible to help you decide what career path would be best. Also let them know that you are enlisting their help to broaden your perspective, so encourage them to be honest with their answers, even if they may seem a little out of the ordinary. Give them the following list of questions before you get together to discuss their thoughts. As them to jot down their answers before you sit down to talk, so that they have to time to think about their answers before talking to you about your own perceptions.

1. What do you see as my overall strengths?

2. What would you say are my most noteworthy, specific skills and talents?

3. What do you consider my biggest opportunities for growth, both personally and professionally?

4. Where do you see me sabotaging myself?

5. What types of jobs/careers strike you as a good fit for me? Why?

As you get the feedback from your friends, keep your mind as open as possible. Try not to immediately accept or reject anything they have to say. Remember, the goal here is to expand the view from your personal window on the world.

You now have gathered a great deal of information, but it is only half of what you need to effectively develop a new career path. The process of changing careers is a little like putting together a jigsaw puzzle. If you only have a few pieces on the table, it is impossible to create the full picture. But once you have all the necessary pieces at your disposal, the final picture starts to come together.

So, turn the page for the rest of the puzzle pieces. . . .

Clarifying Your Values, Passions, and Interests

Most of us try to do our best to live our lives based on what we value and feel to be important. Given the fast pace of our lives and the overwhelming pressure to be successful, however, it can be easy to lose sight of what is important to us. And often it is only when we notice that our lives are completely off balance that we realize we are out of sync with our core values.

Changing careers provides a wonderful opportunity to pause and reexamine what is important to you. Since you are already in the process of making a change in your life, this is a great time to make the adjustments you need to realign your life with your values. In this section I hope to help you clarify your current value set and identify your passions, as well as challenge you to define and embrace your life purpose.

It may be tempting to skip this section, especially if you are not comfortable going inward and turning to your heart and gut for the answers. But I strongly encourage you to stay the course, because the information that you gather here will not only provide the remaining puzzle pieces, it will also help you define the kind of work environment that will be best for you.

VALUES

Before you can set out to define your personal value set, it's important to be clear about what we mean by *value*. It is very easy to lump values together with standards, expectations, and ideals. To do so, however, obscures and dilutes the meaning of all of these concepts, which are in fact distinct from one another.

In the context of this book and your career change, a *value* is a principal or quality that you are committed to living your life in accordance with. Values are not something you aspire to, such as an ideal, nor are they a measure of performance, like a standard. Values are the principals that guide your life, not because of what you hope they will bring you (e.g., success or wealth), but because you believe them to be intrinsically valuable. And a life lived according to those values is by extension also intrinsically valuble.

We assimilate values from different places in our lives, starting with our family; then branching out to friends, teachers, and colleagues; and then our culture. Some of these values we will take as our own—while we may let go of others as we begin to more clearly define who we are and the kind of life we want to live.

As you and your life change, often your values change as well. Events such as getting married, having children, or suffering a major health crisis can easily cause shifts in your values. Thus it is important to take time every now and then to reassess your values and make sure that you are actually living your life in accordance with your values.

The "Identifying Your Values" exercise is designed to help you reexamine your value set and clearly identify the values that are important to you at this point in your life.

One of the biggest reasons for dissatisfaction and conflict in both our personal and professional lives is that we are living our lives in opposition to our core values. If creativity is one of your values, then it will be very important for you to seek out work environments that encourage and support creativity. If you value autonomy, working in an environment that emphasizes teamwork will only frustrate and anger you.

Your values are unique to you, and it is important that you honor them. You will only be at your best for yourself, your family, and your profession if your life and your values are in harmony.

IDENTIFYING YOUR VALUES

1. Review the list of values on the next page and circle the values that you want to guide your personal life. Feel free to add values that aren't listed at the bottom of the page. Remember, values refer to a way of living your life. Values are neither something to strive for, nor something you "should" have. They are the principals that guide the choices you make in life.

2. Now select your top five personal values, list them in the left-hand column of the third page of the workbook, and prioritize them from one to five, with one being the most important. How do you feel when think about those five values? Do you feel that your life pretty well exemplifies these values, or has it gotten out of sync with what you feel to be important?

3. Review the list of values again and place a "W" next to each of the values you hold important in your work. Feel free to write in values that aren't listed at the bottom of the page, flagging each of these with a "W" as well.

4. Now select your top five work values and, once again, prioritize them from one to five. It is likely there may be some overlap between your personal values and your career values, but there also may be some big differences. For example, you may value your intense inner drive at work, but you may be just as happy to leave it at work when you go home.

IDENTIFYING YOUR VALUES (CONT'D)

Values

Achievement	Excellence	Playfulness
Adventure	Excitement	Equality
Affection	Fame	Recognition
Approval	Family	Relaxation
Autonomy	Freedom	Reliability
Beauty	Friendship	Respect
Being right	Fulfillment	Risk
Being the best	Fun/Laughter	Safety
Candor	Happiness	Security
Caring	Hard work	Self-control
Challenge	Health	Self-expression
Change	Honesty	Service
Comfort	Humor	Simplicity
Commitment	Independence	Solitude
Competitiveness	Inner drive	Spiritual development
Connection	Integrity	Spontaneity
Control	Joy	Philanthropy
Cooperation	Justice	Success
Creativity	Knowledge	Truth
Dignity	Leadership	Uniqueness
Effectiveness	Love	Vitality
Elegance	Loyalty	Wealth
Empowerment	Peace	Winning
Enlightenment	Perseverance	Wisdom

Others: _____

_____

IDENTIFYING YOUR VALUES (CONT'D)

Personal Values   **Work Values**

_____   _____

_____   _____

_____   _____

_____   _____

_____   _____

5. Now, for each of your top five values in both lists, ask yourself three questions:

Is this something I truly value or something I want to achieve?

How do I define this value? Example: If you chose loyalty as a value, how do you personally define loyalty?

How can I make sure that I integrate this value into my daily life?

PASSIONS AND INTERESTS

What are you passionate about?

How did you react to that question? On being asked about their passions, some people start creating a mental list of activities and issues that they are passionate about, whereas others may feel a slight sense of anxiety or even resentment because they can't think of anything they are really passionate about.

Passion is a loaded word, and it often comes with an underlying "should." There is a commonly held belief that any intelligent, successful, and caring human being should be able to find at least one thing that they feel passionate about. I would like to challenge that assumption.

Passion is an emotion, and as such people experience it differently. Some of us may have more passion in our mix, while others of us may have more empathy or something else altogether. Some of us were raised in families where expressing ideas passionately was common and encouraged, whereas others of us were raised in families who didn't express strong emotion and were uncomfortable with the energy that passion generates. Still others feel very strongly (and express those feelings) about any number of issues but nevertheleass don't associate the word *passion* with abstract concepts.

If you are someone who has been struggling to identify a passion, relax. Try using a different word instead. For example, I'll wager you have some definite interests or goals. There may be issues and activities you feel strongly about, but not strongly enough for you to consider them passions. Perhaps you associate passion with lack of reason— some dictionary definitions of the word do as well. Whatever the reason for your resistance to the question, the important thing is to give yourself an opportunity to engage your passions and interests to the greatest extent possible for you. There is no single right way to do this. As you relax and enjoy your involvement in whatever activity speaks to you, you may be surprised to find that you can tap into more passion than you knew you had.

Our interests and passions tell us a lot about who we are and how we like to engage with the world. If you love to climb mountains, you probably like to challenge yourself, enjoy the serenity of nature, and maybe enjoy solitude or the camaraderie of a few close friends. If your passion is eliminating homelessness, you probably enjoy working with others, problem solving, and community organizing.

Some people are fortunate enough to integrate their passions and interests with their work. Depending on your particular interests and the role you want work to play in your life, it may or may not be possible for you to integrate your passion into your work. But if you are clear about the characteristics you want to incorporate in your work, then you will be better able to choose a work environment that will offer the elements most important to you.

The "Passions and Interests" exercise will help you identify your passions and interests and begin to see how elements of these might be translated to your work environment. Complete the exercise before moving on to the next section.

FINDING PURPOSE IN YOUR LIFE

Up to this point, you have been gathering information about your skills, talents, passions, interests, and values to help you get a clearer sense of the types of careers might be most satisfying for you. Your focus has been inward, looking at how you can enhance your life.

In this section, your focus is going to shift outward. Taking the information you have gathered, you are now going to look at how you can combine your skills and values to give to the world in a way that holds meaning to you. As you begin thinking in terms of contributing to others, you will be taking the first steps toward finding purpose in your life.

PASSIONS AND INTERESTS

1. In the first column, list of all the activities, issues, and concerns that touch your heart and light your fire. These are your passions or interests.

2. Do you see common characteristics? Do you like doing things by yourself or with others? Do you like to push yourself or do you like activities that are more relaxing? List any common themes that you notice in the second column.

3. Now, circle your top three items. What do these three things have in common? What is it about each of these activities/issues that excites and motivates you? As things come to mind, jot them down.

4. Taking the information gathered, list the top three characteristics from your passions/interests that you want to make sure are part of your next job. For example, problem solving, autonomy, creativity, or nature. Highlight these characteristics. This is important information for you as you begin planning your new career path.

Passions/Interests	Common Themes	Top Three Characteristics

Having purpose in your life is what gives it meaning. Being successful and accomplishing the goals you set for yourself can be very satisfying, but it's not the kind of satisfaction that brings long-term fulfillment. Finding a purpose, and living your life from that purpose, changes the way you view the world. Purpose gives meaning to your life and enables you to experience the joy that comes from knowing you, in your own way, are contributing to the greater good of the world.

That said, the fact remains that discussion of life purpose elicits anxiety in many people, much as the subject of passion does. There is the suggestion that you should know what your purpose is. There is the suggestion that your life purpose should create significant change in the world. And there is the suggestion that your singular life purpose is floating around somewhere in the universe just waiting for you to discover it.

Finding purpose in your life is not a mystical process. In fact, for most of us it is an intentional process. We can define our own purpose. Having purpose means being committed to a value, principle, or belief that gives your life meaning and compels you to take action that contributes to the greater good. Gandhi defined it very clearly when he said, "Be the change you want to see in the world."

You can find your purpose in your work. You may choose to provide the best customer service possible by bringing respect, honesty, and integrity to every client interaction. You can find purpose in your passions. If your passion is painting, you may decide to provide free artwork for the senior citizen center. And you can find purpose in the combination of your work and passions. If your passion is nature, you may choose to work for an environmental organization that is dedicated to preserving old growth forests.

Why is it important to find purpose in your life? Having a purpose raises your awareness and expands the way you think about yourself in the world. It allows you to step outside the ordinary confines of your life and experience a greater connection with the world. It gives you the opportunity to contribute to the world in your own way, and it brings you a sense of joy and fulfillment that you can only experience by focusing on something greater than just your life.

I encourage you to take the time to think about what change you want to be in the world. Your purpose does not have to be of epic proportions. You never know how changing the life of one person could change the world.

Your values, passions, and purpose are what make you the unique person you are. They are your guiding principles. As you read the next section on work environments, keep the information you have just gathered in the back of your mind. Knowing what is important to you and being aware of how you want to interact with the world will help you more clearly define the work environment that will best support you.

CAREER STAGE

People change careers for different reasons depending on where they are professionally. If you are at the beginning of your professional life and want to change careers, you are most likely looking for a career that will advance your professional standing. At this point, your primary focus is on doing and achieving. You are anxious to learn as much as possible in as many different areas as possible. You may decide to go back to school. Anything is possible. Obstacles don't exist. For you, success is defined by what you know, what you achieve, and how far up the career ladder you can climb. Being at this stage in your career development can make it easier to find new jobs. Your major requirement is the chance to learn and grow professionally, and there are many job opportunities that will fit this criterion.

However, if you are in the middle of your professional life, you are likely to view work from a very different perspective. The idealism and energy that propelled you through the first 10 or 15 years of your professional life have likely been replaced by a keen sense of realism.

You have worked hard and have mastered a wide array of business skills. You have accomplished most of your professional goals and would describe yourself as successful except for the fact that you feel something is missing. Your relationship with work has changed. Work no longer holds the excitement and challenge it used to. You find that your focus has shifted from wanting to achieve to wanting to be more fulfilled in your work life.

If you are changing careers in this stage of your professional life, you will be looking for a career that will hold more meaning for you and that will be more closely aligned with your interests and values. It will be important that what you do contributes in some way to the greater good and enlivens and enriches your life.

This shift from seeking mastery to seeking meaning in your work is a natural step in one's professional life. Yet, not everyone will listen to their hearts and make the move to find a new and more fulfilling career. People will find all sorts of reasons why they couldn't or shouldn't leave their current jobs, even though they are no longer happy, challenged, or satisfied in their work.

Some will stay because they think it is the right and professional thing to do. Some will stay because they are afraid to step outside their comfort zone. And some will stay because they don't believe that they deserve to follow their dreams.

Working in a situation that no longer feeds you personally or professionally serves no one. Your dissatisfaction with your professional life influences not only your work, but it also ripples out and affects your friends, family, and colleagues. When you are prevented from being everything you can be, everyone around you, including you, suffers.

So, allow yourself to follow your heart and seek out a career that is better aligned with your interests and values and that will bring meaning and excitement back into your professional life.

Your work is to discover your work and then with all your heart to give yourself to it.
   —Buddha

Defining Your Ideal Work Environment

It can be easy to look at your job only in terms of your specific responsibilities and forget that the working environment is a significant contributor to overall job satisfaction. Often, it's only when a problem arises that you begin to consider your environment. You become aware of the things you don't like, and when you think about looking for another job, you make sure that those elements are not part of the environment at your new job.

But that doesn't guarantee that you will land in an environment that does work for you. It merely ensures you have eliminated those issues. There may be many other things you don't like in your new environment. Therefore, this approach is not the best way to find a supportive work environment.

A more effective strategy is to take time before you start looking for a job to define your ideal work environment. There are two benefits to doing this research. First, you will have the information you need to make intelligent and informed decisions about future jobs. Second, becoming more aware about the types of environments that appeal to you may spark new ideas about what you want to be doing. For example, if you come to realize that you really love being outside, you may start thinking about how you could bring your skills to environmental work.

There are many factors to take into consideration when you think about the work environment. Some are obvious, such as work space and location, whereas others can be more subtle, such as the levels of noise and natural light.

The following list of questions will help you define your ideal work environment:

1. Do you want to work in a specific geographical area?

2. Do you like working inside or outside? City or suburbs?

3. Do you want to work for yourself or for an organization?

4. What type of organization would you be most comfortable working for (large corporation, medium or small business, nonprofit, government)?

5. Describe your ideal office space (light, space, privacy, etc.).

6. How much do you want to interact with other people on a daily basis?

7. What types of people do you enjoy working with?

8. Are you more comfortable working as part of a team or by yourself?

9. What do you need from a supervisor to perform at your best?

10. How much structure do you need to your day? What does that structure look like?

11. How much responsibility and decision-making power do you want to have?

12. Do you want to travel for work?

13. How many hours a week are you willing to work?

14. How do you want to be recognized and rewarded at work?

15. How important is it that your core values and beliefs are congruent with those of the organization you work for?

16. List any other characteristics that you may have thought of.

As you think about these questions, be completely honest in your answers. Don't censor yourself because you think that you will never be able to get what you want or that what you want is in some way unreasonable or irresponsible. For one thing, no one will see your answers unless you want them to. And your answers will give you a great deal of useful information about what you value in your workplace. And when you know what you want, you can proactively seek it out instead of reactively bouncing from place to place hoping to find it.

The last four sections have given you a lot of information. You have identified the skills and talents you want to continue using. You know which competencies you want to develop. You are more aware of the values that guide your personal and professional life, and you have a clearer sense of the kind of work environment that suits you. You have collected all the pieces to your puzzle. It is now time to put all this information together and begin thinking creatively about the career path(s) you want to pursue.

Identifying Your Dream Job

If you can dream it, you can do it.
　　—Walt Disney

There are two ways to approach the task of transitioning to a new job. The first, and most common, approach is to think about the jobs you have held in the past and then search for positions that require a similar skill set and knowledge base. With this approach you know you can do the job and you know that you can appropriately edit your resume to at least get your foot in the door. All in all, you feel pretty comfortable about applying for positions that meet this description.

The upside to this approach is that it doesn't require much time, thought, or preparation on your part. The road you are traveling is familiar and safe. Because you've had experience in similar positions and you have the skills and abilities the company is looking for, chances are good that you will at least be brought in for an interview.

The downside to this approach is that it doesn't involve much time, thought, or preparation on your part. And, while you save a lot of time and effort on not looking for a job that meets your needs, you then have to package yourself and your skills to meet the employer's needs. Your focus is on trying to please the employer; in doing that, you are giving up some of your power in the interaction. As a result, you will likely end up settling for something that is okay, rather than something that really sparks your interest and challenges your abilities. In short, you are selling yourself short.

The second approach, the one outlined in this book, is much more proactive. With this approach, you design the ideal job for you, and then you go out and actively search for the position that best matches your criteria. The downside is that this approach takes more time and effort. It also requires that you take a risk and step into your power, which can be difficult for many people. (However, as you get more comfortable with the concept of personal power, this becomes a benefit!)

The biggest upside to this approach is that you are much more likely to end up in a career that is professionally challenging and personally fulfilling because you are engaging in the process on your own terms. This is a much more empowering approach. Going for something that you truly want also instills an energy, focus, and confidence that will work to your benefit when you begin talking with potential employers.

THINKING CREATIVELY

When you decide to make a change in your life, you are deciding to do something new. Doing something new involves creative thinking and a willingness to look beyond the status quo.

We all live our lives in our own little boxes. Although these boxes may be confining, they are familiar to us. Our boxes offer us a limited window from which we see the world. Every day we look at the same thing, and eventually we come to believe that what we see is the way that all of life is. When you decided to change careers, you made a conscious decision to enlarge the window on your world. You are giving yourself permission to think creatively and to step outside your box.

Some people appear to be better at thinking creatively than others. You may be someone who has no problem thinking of new ideas and possibilities. If that's the case, it is very likely that you will be totally energized by changing careers because there are so many new and exciting possibilities bouncing around in your head.

But what if you aren't as comfortable with the creative thought process? What if you get nervous when you think about all the possibilities; or worse, what happens when you can't think of any possibilities? If this describes you, I would invite you to look carefully at the beliefs you are holding onto about how creative you are.

We all have the ability to be creative. Some of us have the good fortune to have people in our lives who have encouraged us to embrace our creative side, thus helping us to develop a confidence and comfort with the creative process. Unfortunately, others of us have had people in our lives who, for whatever reason, have taken it on themselves to squelch any attempts we have made to be creative. As a result we have come to believe that we have no creative ability. The truth is, we all have the ability to think creatively. We just need the opportunity to develop trust and confidence in that ability.

If you feel you need some help jump-starting your creative flow, try one or more of these simple activities:

1. Spend some time playing with a toddler.

2. Go dancing.

3. Take a walk in nature.

4. Rearrange or paint a room in your house.

5. Take a daily task and do it differently everyday for a week.

6. Listen to inspiring music.

7. Take 15 minutes each day to sit quietly by yourself.

8. Do some writing—journaling, stories, poetry, etc.

9. Visit an art gallery, museum, or aquarium.

10. Take a class in something you have never done before.

The process of changing something in your life gives you the opportunity to get reacquainted with your creative side. So, don't be afraid venture outside your box and explore all the possibilities that are available.

DESIGNING YOUR DREAM JOB

Listen to your dreams—those are the sounds no one else can hear.
    —Kobi Yamada

At this point you may be wondering how creating a make-believe job is going to help you find a new career. The goal of the exercise on the next page is to help you think creatively about career possibilities. It can be very easy to limit your scope to only what you think you should do, to what you think is acceptable, or to what your logical mind is telling you is possible. Using your imagination and creativity will help you see new things and to connect the dots in different ways. You will become more aware of how many of the skills you have are transferable, and this realization will open up all sorts of new opportunities for you.

Being free to put your dreams down on paper encourages you to think more from your heart and less from the logical place in your mind. As a result, your ideal job will hold a great deal of information about what you truly enjoy doing and may help you realize that there are some significant changes you want to make as you head for a new career.

For example, your ideal job may have you working for yourself, something that you have not seriously contemplated before. But as you develop this job, you begin to see that working for yourself could be a real possibility. Your thinking begins to shift and you start to look at your next career from a whole new perspective.

Or maybe the job you create isn't as high powered as you thought it would be, and you begin to realize that your values have changed and that quality of life and work/life balance are more important to you now than money and prestige. Perhaps you realize that your quest for money and prestige doesn't reflect your values and has instead put you on the fast track to burnout. This kind of realization can be very freeing and will help ensure your next job is more in line with your values.

There is also another reason for doing this exercise. Being able to freely create a perfect job scenario that includes all characteristics you need and want will dramatically increase your probability of finding that job, or one very similar. This happens more frequently that you might imagine. But it will only happen if you know what you are looking for, if you are willing to go after it, and if you believe in your ability to achieve it.

Contrary to what you may think, there is nothing wrong with going for your dreams. If you fall short, you will still end up far ahead of where you would have been had you not tried at all. This is your life and you've got one shot at it. Why not make it the best it can be?

 YOUR DREAM JOB

Using the information you have gathered in the previous sections, design your perfect job. Be as creative in this process as possible. What would you absolutely love to do? Describe as many elements of your dream job as possible and be as specific as you can. Remember, this is your ideal. There are no restrictions.

What industry are you working in?

_____

What position do you have?

_____

_____

What are your job responsibilities?

_____

_____

_____

YOUR DREAM JOB (CONT'D)

Describe your work environment.

_____

_____

_____

What kinds of people are you working with?

_____

_____

_____

How much money are you making?

_____

How many hours a week do you work?

_____

What kind of boss do you have?

_____

_____

_____

YOUR DREAM JOB (CONT'D)

What's the best thing about this job?

_____

_____

_____

I hope that this exercise has helped you generate some new ideas about career possibilities, as well as helped you think about your old ideas from a broader perspective. Maybe you have discovered a brand new career idea that you want to pursue, or maybe you have several ideas that you want to check out. It is now time for you to take action and start moving toward your new career.

Developing an Action Plan

When trying to make a change, many people struggle with translating their ideas into action. In their heads, the ideas make a lot of sense, and they can see all sorts of ways to implement them; yet when it comes to actually taking the steps needed to make things happen, everything falls apart.

One way to avoid this pitfall is to develop an effective action plan. An effective action plan includes well-defined goals, viable action steps, and a realistic timeline. The clearer your plan of action, the better your chances of reaching your goals. In this section you will develop a plan of action that will provide the vision, structure, and timeline you will need to reach your goals.

The first step in developing an action plan is to define your goal. Is it to find a job in a specific industry? Is it to find a job that will financially support you? Is it to be living a life that is congruent with your values? What do you want from this process? What will success look like to you?

For some of you, the answers to these questions will be very focused. You know the direction you are heading and the career path you are choosing. Others of you are going to be more general in your response. You have a sense of what you want out of your next career; you are just not sure which career path will give you what you want. Wherever you are in this spectrum is fine. Just try to articulate as clearly as possible what you are striving for. Following are some examples of goals that reflect the different places people might be in this process:

1. To successfully transition from a career in high-tech to starting my own consulting company.

2. To be working in a career that incorporates my love of nature.

3. To be working in a career that financially supports me and that is congruent with my purpose and values.

Having a goal gives you a starting place and a framework from which to work. As you talk with people, do research, and find out more about various careers, it will be easier for you to make decisions because you know what you want the outcome to be.

Once you have a goal in place, the next step is to identify the specific actions you need to take to ensure you achieve that goal. You may feel overwhelmed because you either don't know how to get started or you see too many things to do and don't know which one to do first. Either scenario can result in feeling very stuck.

The best way to get unstuck in any situation is to do something. To get started, make a list of all of information you need to begin developing an action strategy. You may have general questions about a certain industry. You may need to research the skills needed for certain jobs, or you may need to do research about the costs and availability of training or educational programs. Or maybe you are concerned about having enough support to get you through this process.

When you have your list completed, go through it and after each item, write down the best place to find that piece of information. Common sources of information include friends, the library, the Internet, or informational interviews. (Informational interviews are discussed in the next chapter.)

Once you are finished with that step, go back through the list and prioritize the questions you need answered first. For example if you find you can't afford the cost of a specific training program, there is no real need to conduct informational interviews in that field.

Once you have your list prioritized, you can begin creating action steps for each item. I suggest you take the first five items on the list and create action steps for each one. Once you have completed those actions, you can go back and repeat this process with the next five items on the list.

There are two reasons for taking five items at a time. First, you don't want to become completely overwhelmed by having too much to do. Second, as you gather different pieces of information, some of the questions lower down on your list may become irrelevant or increase in importance. This process is not linear. As you move forward, different doors will open and different possibilities will arise. As this happens, you may find your direction shifting and there may be new issues and questions to address.

When you create an action step, make it as specific as possible. The purpose of action steps is to facilitate the change process and to help you reach your goal more quickly and easily. Following are examples of some actions steps one might take to achieve the stated goal:

Goal: To successfully transition from a career in business to owning my own massage practice.

Action Step 1: Research different massage schools in the area regarding cost, time, etc.

Action Step 2: Set up a coffee date with Kim to discuss how she started her massage business, the costs, the problems, etc.

Action Step 3: Put together a budget that includes the costs of training and start-up to make sure the idea is financially feasible for me.

Action Step 4: Schedule interviews with the different schools to decide which would be best for me.

Action Step 5: Interview three life coaches to decide whether I want to work with a coach to facilitate this process.

As clear as action steps may be, they are not going to be of any value to you unless you implement them. So, to help make sure that happens, you need to develop a timeline.

There are two basic ways to create a timeline. One is to allot a total time to the entire transition process and then work backwards. Say for example you've decided to give yourself 6 months to transition to a new career. Knowing that you have a 6-month framework will allow you to set due dates for each of your action steps accordingly.

Another method is to set due dates for each group of action steps and not to worry about having a definitive end date. This method works well for people who aren't in a hurry but who are self-starters who can keep themselves motivated.

Each person's organizational skills and relationship to time is different, so it is important for you to chose the method works best for you. As I stated earlier, this process is not a linear one, and it can be easy to get bogged down or veer off course. But having an effective time management strategy in place will help you avoid many of these common obstacles so that you can keep moving toward your goal.

The preparations for your journey are now complete. You have gathered the information you need, you have created a viable action plan, and you have a support network of people standing by to help out as needed. All the pieces are in place, and you are ready to start your journey!

Beginning Your Journey

Sailing Through the Fog of Transition

Implementing Your Action Plan

Overcoming Common Obstacles

Staying the Course

The Light at the End of the Tunnel

Sailing Through the Fog of Transition

If one advances confidently in the direction of his dreams, and endeavors to live the life which he has imagined, he will meet with a success unexpected in common hours.
    —Henry David Thoreau

You have developed your goal and you have action steps in place to ensure that you reach that goal. It is now time to move from ideas to action. This chapter will serve as your guide as you begin the transition process to your new career.

To fully understand the transition process, it is important to understand the difference between a *change* and a *transition*. A change occurs when something starts or stops in your life and something else takes its place. For example, quitting your job is a change. Getting hired into a new position is another change.

Transition, on the other hand, is the psychological process that you go through to let go of an old identity (old job) and take on a new identity (new job). Transition involves leaving behind a life that you knew and moving toward a life that is unknown and uncertain. Whereas change is a single action, transition is a process that unfolds over time.

I compare going through a transition to setting sail on a foggy sea. As you begin your transition, you can still see the shoreline. At this point, you may not even realize that you are in a transition. You are very excited about all the possibilities waiting for you, and you can hardly wait to explore the distant shores.

Yet, as you sail further out to sea, or further into your transition, you lose sight of the familiar shoreline. The fog begins to settle in around you. You can't make out where you are going and you can no longer see where you came from. This feeling of drifting at sea with no port in sight is unnerving. We live in a culture that demands fast and definitive answers to our questions. We want quick solutions to our problems. We want fast and easy ways out of the fog.

So when you find yourself in the middle of this kind of uncertainty, it can be very easy to give in to the discomfort of not knowing exactly where you are going or if the course you've chosen is the right one for you. You may begin to question your decision to change careers, and you will probably begin to hear the voice of self-doubt telling you you've made a mistake and that you really don't have what it takes to make it through the fog. You notice your resolve slipping away, and at this point you may think about quitting the journey and returning to the comfort of the old and familiar shoreline.

But if you let the voices of fear and doubt override the voices coming from your heart, you are apt to make decisions about your future that will not serve you well in the long run. The decisions you make when you are feeling scared will most likely move your life backward, because in trying to soothe your fear and anxiety, it is only logical to seek the comfort and security of what you know.

However, it is at this point in your journey, when you are feeling the most scared and unsure that you need to put your full trust in the transition process. You need to believe that if you keep yourself open to the experience and if you continue to take small steps toward your goal, you will eventually sail out of the fog and find yourself in a new and exciting career.

Staying one's course in the midst of confusion and doubt can be difficult, but there are some things you can do to avoid getting knocked off course. The first is to understand that transition is a process with its own inherent set of ups and downs and that feelings of doubt and disorientation are a normal part of the process. The more you are aware of what to expect, the better able you will be to deal with the uncertainties.

Second, don't be afraid to use your support system as you go through this process. When your confidence begins to wane, think about what you need to get back on track and then call the person on your support team who could best fill that need. You may just need some encouragement. You may want some help thinking of better ways to stay motivated. Or you may just need to go to a movie and forget all of this for a couple of hours. Whatever you need, give yourself permission to ask for help. This need not be a solo journey.

And finally, remember that slow and steady will win this race. Listen to the voice in your heart, not the gremlins in your head. And always keep your dream in front of you as a beacon guiding you through the fog.

Implementing Your Action Plan

Implementing your action plan is the beginning of your journey, and the effectiveness of your implementation plan will have a significant impact the quality of your overall journey. This section will help you put structures in to place that will allow for a smooth and efficient implementation.

TIMELINES

One of the best ways to keep you on track when working on a project of this size is to create timelines using time-management strategies that will work best for you.

The first question to address as you develop your timeline is how long you want to dedicate to your career search. Your answer to this question will depend on many factors. The first thing to consider is the scope of what you are trying to achieve. If you know that you want to leave your job as a financial advisor and start your own consulting business, your focus is pretty clear and you know what specific steps you need to take to reach your goals.

But if your goal is to find a career that is meaningful, that will provide financial security, and that will allow you to use your creative skills, you are starting with a much broader focus that will have many more options. As a result, you may want to allow yourself more time to reach your goal.

Next there is the financial consideration. If you are going to be employed through this transition, this may not be a factor. But if you are out of work, or if you are soon going to be out of work, it is important to think about how long you can comfortably live without a steady income. You don't want to deal with the extra pressures of financial stress as you are trying to focus on your action steps.

The third issue to consider is how anxious are you to change careers. Are you extremely unhappy in your current position and want to make a change as quickly as possible? Or maybe you are just considering a change and going through this process to gather more information so that you can consider all your options before making any decisions.

And finally, you need to consider what kind of time frame suits your personal style. Are you someone who is very action-oriented and who works best under a little pressure? Or do you prefer taking your time with things? The key here is to find the pace that keeps you moving forward without putting too much pressure on you and without giving you so much leeway that you lose your focus and interest. Only you know what the right pace for you is.

Once you have taken all this information into consideration, choose a time frame that makes the best sense to you. It may be 3 months, or 6 months, or even 24 months.

If you are someone who is driven to achieve, add a month to your timeline. This is a process that requires not only action, but also thought and contemplation, to be successful. Therefore, it is important to give yourself that extra cushion of time to be able to process the information you get and the decisions you have to make along the way. If you are someone who is laid-back, who takes your time to get things done, subtract 1 month from your timeline. This will give you a little extra incentive to stay focused and moving forward.

WEEKLY GOALS

One of the most effective ways to reach your destination in the time you have allotted is to create weekly schedules. Each week, choose one or two action items that you want to accomplish. It is important to keep your number of action steps for each week low so that you will have a higher likelihood of completing them. It can be tempting, particularly at the beginning of this process, to take on five items at once. You are very excited about getting started and want to do as much as possible.

But unfortunately life usually gets in the way of your good intentions and you won't be able to finish all your tasks. This will leave you feeling discouraged and can cause you to lose momentum. You are much more likely to experience success when you keep your list short; and being successful will give you the confidence to keep moving toward your dream.

Working from a weekly schedule also gives you the opportunity to constantly adjust your course of action. As you gather more information, you may find new doors opening, new ideas popping up, or new opportunities presenting themselves. When this happens, it only makes sense to revise your plan. You may want to eliminate some of the original items on your list and add others. Using a weekly schedule will allow you to react to these changes more quickly, thus saving you time and energy in the long run.

Once you have decided on your items for the week, schedule specific time on your calendar to work on them. If you are going to call someone to set up a meeting, write the call in your appointment book. If you need to do some research, block off some time for that. If possible choose times that are not sandwiched between intense meetings or activities. Give yourself some space so that you can really focus on the task at hand.

You will likely feel more comfortable doing some tasks and less comfortable with others. When this occurs, it is best to schedule the difficult task early in the week so that you can get it out of the way. Then move on to the task that is more fun. That way you will end the week on a positive note, and you will have the energy and motivation to tackle the next week's projects.

Schedule a specific time each week for creating your schedule. Once you have it completed, post it somewhere where you will see it often. There is a great deal of validity to the old saying, "Out of sight, out of mind." So, do whatever it takes to remind you to take action. Draw your schedule in color and post it on your mirror, refrigerator, or wall at work. Put it on your computer calendar, with a reminder. Tell your friends what you are working on and ask for friendly reminders.

Weeks can go by quickly, and unless you stay focused and on task, it can be very easy to let things slide. And once that happens, it can be very difficult to get up and running again. But if you can keep moving ahead at a steady pace, you will be surprised at how quickly you will reach your destination.

FINDING THE INFORMATION YOU NEED

Asking the Right Questions

One of the biggest hurdles to successfully implementing your action plan can be figuring out where to find information. The simple fact is, the more information you have, the easier it is going to be for you to make informed decisions. But it can be overwhelming to try and figure out where to get the answers you need or even which questions to ask.

Before you can get the information you're actually looking for, you need to know the right questions to ask. There are several different ways of addressing an issue, and depending on the question you choose to ask, you will get different responses. So, it is important to be very clear about the information you want and to ask the questions that will elicit that information.

Say, for example, that you are thinking about becoming a real estate agent. You want to know more about real estate, so you set up meetings with a couple of your friends who are agents. Here are two different types of questions you might ask.

Closed Questions

1. Do you like your job?

2. How many hours a week do you work?

3. How long does it take to become licensed?

4. How long did it take to get your business really up and running?

Open-Ended Questions

1. What do you really like about being in real estate? What don't you like about it?

2. How many hours per week do you work? How have you been able to schedule your work so that you are not on call 24/7?

3. How long does it take to get licensed? Tell me about the process.

4. What are some of the difficulties you ran into when you started out?

5. What do you think it takes to be a successful as a real estate agent? What do you consider the main reasons that some people aren't successful?

Clearly, the second set of questions will elicit more useful information than the first set. People typically only answer the questions asked. So, if you ask closed questions, the answers will be brief. But if you ask more open-ended questions, people will give you more information. Also, open-ended questions are softer and more engaging, and more likely to initiate a conversation, as opposed to a survey.

You can use this same technique when you ask questions of yourself to make sure that you get useful information instead of the usual general response. For example, let's say you are considering the possibility of moving to another city for your career. Instead of asking yourself, Do I want to move to San Francisco?, ask yourself questions such as, What are the pros and cons of moving?, or Why am I hesitant about moving?

These kinds of questions will get to the root of the issue and provide the kind of information that will facilitate your decision-making process.

Locating Information Sources

Now that you have a better idea of the kinds of questions to ask, where should you look for information? You are one source, and the external world is the other source. There will be some questions that only you know the answers to, such as, Should I move?, Should I go back to school?, or How much money do I want to make? Though you may ask other people for their opinions, the final decision is up to you. It is important to accept this responsibility, because it can be easy to let other people make or heavily influence your decisions. You are the only one who knows what is right for you, so it is likely that following someone else's advice is not going to take you where you want to go.

For the rest of the information you need, turn to the resources in the external world, which can be divided into two categories: places and people. Sometimes you will need to find up-to-date facts or basic information about a career. Maybe you need to research the requirements to get into a specific graduate school or training program. Or maybe you want information about the potential growth rate in a certain field. This type of information can be found at the library, on the Internet, or in trade publications, for example. These resources can give you the latest research and information on all careers, and will provide a good starting place for your initial inquiries.

The other external source of information is people. People have an amazing amount of information to share if you are willing to ask. Your friends, family, and professional colleagues are a good starting place. Talk with them about your plans. Ask them questions and bounce ideas off of them. They will give you names of people to talk with. As you talk with these new people, they also will know people. Doors will open and opportunities will arise. This is person-to-person networking and it is one of the best ways of collecting information for a career transition.

The Informational Interview

The ultimate person-to-person networking tool is the informational interview. An informational interview involves talking with people who are currently working in a field to gain a better understanding of an occupation or industry. Informational interviews provide an opportunity to ask all the questions you have about a specific industry, to get a second-hand look at the work environment, and to gain a good sense of whether you would fit into this type of work setting. They can also give you the perfect opportunity to practice your interview skills in a less stressful environment, thus building your confidence for job interviews.

But one of the best things about conducting informational interviews is that you gain visibility. You are demonstrating your skills, interests, talents, and passions in the questions you ask and the way you engage in conversation. You are talking with a potential employer and through your conversation they will gain a sense of you who are and what you could bring to the workplace. Even if they don't have an appropriate opening in their office, they may know of other jobs that would be a good fit for you and give you names of other people to talk with. More doors will open and more opportunities will present themselves.

It can be intimidating to set up your first informational interview, especially if you don't have a name of a specific person at the company. However, if you call the company and explain why you are calling and what you are looking for, most receptionists will know who you should talk to. If they don't, ask to speak to someone in human resources. And the good news is that most people love to talk about their job and their organization and will be very willing to sit down with you and answer your questions. Once you have conquered the first interview, the rest will be a breeze.

To get the most out of your interview time, think about what you want to ask and write your questions out in advance. Remember to use open-ended questions.

Make sure the list is not too long, but that it captures the essential points of information that you want. Here are some examples of questions you might ask:

- What are the duties/responsibilities of your job?

- What do you find most satisfying and most frustrating about your job?

- Do you feel your work is important and meaningful?

- What is a typical day like?

- How would you describe the work environment?

- What kinds of interaction do you have with peers, colleagues, supervisors, etc.?

- What are the opportunities for growth?

- What is the best way to get into this field?

- What kind of support is available?

- What sort of compensation could one expect?

- What kinds of people experience the greatest success in this field?

- If you were ever to leave this job, what would be the reason?

Your questions will differ depending on who you are talking with and what you want to learn. One interview may be for collecting factual data, while the next may be to understand the subtleties of a particular workplace or occupation. As you conduct more of these interviews, you will become very skilled at preparing and asking questions.

A great way to get first-hand information about different careers is to volunteer or do an internship in the field of your interest. No matter how much research you do or how many people you talk to about a certain field, there is no substitute for having the opportunity to actually work in the field. Being able to experience the work environment from the inside will give you a much more accurate picture of what the field is like and what certain jobs entail. Volunteering can also be a very good way to test the waters before you jump in and spend a lot of time and money applying to graduate school.

Remember, the more information you get, the better able you will be to make informed decisions about your next career step. All of the information you need is available to you if you have the tenacity and willingness to pursue it. Don't let temporary impatience and frustration steer you off course.

At this point your journey is well underway. You have structures in place to keep you moving forward. You know where to look for the information you need. You have a process in place that will allow for course adjustment as needed. You are moving forward toward your goal.

Overcoming Common Obstacles

Obstacles are frightful things you see when you take your eyes off your goal.
  —Henry Ford

No matter how well prepared you are for this journey, you will encounter at least a few obstacles along the way. You are making a big change in your life. As discussed, all systems resist change, and human systems are no exception. It stands to reason then that you will experience some resistance as you go through this transition.

Resistance can take many forms and can be difficult to identify if you are not consciously watching for it. It usually shows up a few weeks after you've started doing something new. This is when your system realizes that the change you are embarking on may be permanent. Resistance starts quietly by sending out subtle messages to get you to return to your old way of being. If the subtle messages don't work, the bigger guns come out. You simply cannot avoid resistance altogether. But there are ways to deal with it effectively.

PROCRASTINATION

The most effective way to handle resistance is to be aware of it. Remember that resistance is inevitable, but far from insurmountable.

Let's say that you have a list of three people to call for informational interviews. You sit down to make the calls, but decide that you should check your e-mail first. As you are checking your e-mail, you remember that you need to transfer some money into your checking account. So, after reading your e-mail, you log on to your bank's website and take care of your banking. You return to the task of calling and your phone rings. It's a friend who has just returned from a wonderful trip, so you talk for a while and catch up on everything your friend has been doing. After you hang up, you realize that you have a few minutes before your next meeting, so you decide to do the calls tomorrow.

This is a subtle version of resistance. You can easily rationalize why you didn't get to the calls. You have other things that needed to be taken care of. But if you examine it closely, the real issue becomes what caused you to divert your attention from the calls to checking your e-mail in the first place. You were experiencing resistance in its more subtle form. It was sending out just enough fear, doubt, or anxiety to cause you to divert your attention to something easier and more comfortable.

If you are not aware of what happened, you are likely to think that you just got distracted. You couldn't really help it if your friend called, right? But there will always be things to distract you from moving forward into new and uncharted waters. If you know what to look for, you will not be as easily diverted.

SELF-DOUBT

But let's say that you didn't fall for the subtle tactics. You made your calls and scheduled the interviews. The resistance is likely to crank up a notch because you are moving too fast. You may begin to doubt yourself, asking, "Why are you even doing this interview? You will never get hired." Or, "Why are you bothering this person with your trivial questions?" Or, "This is just a waste of time; you didn't get much from the last interview."

These doubts can very persuasive and the louder they become, the more fear you feel and the harder it is to keep moving forward. The first step in not allowing yourself to be manipulated by self-doubt is to be aware of it. Pay attention to how often the voice of self-doubt tells you that you are not good enough, smart enough, or strong enough to do whatever it is you want, as well as how easy it can be to accept the judgments of these voices as fact.

But they are not your true voice. They are coming from the very small part of you who doesn't want to change, and they are doing everything in their power to keep you from moving forward. When you find yourself believing what the voices are saying, don't try to argue with them. They will always win!

Instead, take a few minutes to sit quietly by yourself and try to reconnect with the part of you who has the dream, who wants to try something different, and who has the courage to step outside the box and explore new lands. This is where you will find your power. The critical voices will still play their same old tune. But the more you are able to draw on the feelings of excitement, energy, and adventure that propelled you into this change, the less influence those voices will have.

BUT, WHAT IF . . . ?

Another form of internal resistance is what I call the *what-if jitters*. The what-if jitters replace the harsh voices of self-doubt with voices of indecision, which say things like this:

- What if I make the wrong decision?

- What if I can't do this?

- What if something better comes along?

- What if I make a mistake?

You begin mentally pacing back and forth between your options worrying about the future effects of a decision you haven't even made yet. You are focused so intensely on the future that you can't see the opportunities that are in front of you right now. You are paralyzed by indecision. The system is happy because you are no longer in change mode; but you are left feeling unhappy and discouraged because the only decision you made was not to make any decision.

Once again, the first step to avoiding this trap is to realize when you start to get caught up in the what-if scenario. When you notice it happening, take a minute to see whether you can identify the specific fear or doubt that is underneath. You may be afraid of hurting someone's feelings, for example. Once you realize what the issue is, you can bring it out in the open and deal with it. You may talk to the person and explain what is going on. You might learn they wouldn't be hurt at all, which would be great. Or maybe they will be hurt, but you will have a chance to talk the issue through with them and then move on.

These kinds of fears and uncertainties only keep you stuck when they reside in the recesses of your mind. When they are brought out into the open, they lose their power and you are free to get on with your life.

Fear is a powerful and uncomfortable emotion that can easily slip into your life and take control over what you do and don't do. The important thing to understand about fear is that it is future-based. It gains its power when you begin creating scenarios about what might happen in the future. If you keep your focus on what's happening now, fear will have nothing to attach itself to because, at the moment, all is fine. It's only when you begin thinking about the what-ifs that fear can exist. As Mark Twain said, "I have spent most of my life worrying about things that have never happened."

FEELING STUCK

Another obstacle that you may encounter during your career transition is the experience of feeling stuck. Feeling stuck is different from the paralysis induced by the what-if jitters. You feel stuck when you think you have come to a dead end. Maybe after conducting an informational interview, the career you thought was the right one turned out to be all wrong. Maybe you find that the more information you gather, the more confused you are. Your forward motion has come to an abrupt halt and you do not know how to get restarted.

Stuck is a powerful word. When something is stuck, it cannot move. Describing yourself as stuck sends an unconscious message to your mind that it is not possible for you to make any kind of move. Using the word *stuck* takes away your power.

But, when you look at your situation more closely, you realize you can move. You just aren't sure at this point what the best direction would be. You are not stuck—you are just momentarily stopped.

To get restarted you need to take some sort of action. You might want to call a friend and explain your situation and ask for some encouragement. You might want to take a walk and clear your head. You might want to look at your action plan and revise the focus. Taking any kind of action will get you moving again, while sitting and worrying about how stuck you are will only drag you deeper into the dilemma.

There are many opportunities to get pulled off course in this transition process. It can be very easy to fall victim to the subtle tricks of resistance and let the fears and anxieties of an uncertain future convince you that what you are doing is too hard, and that it would be better to give up your silly dream and return to the familiar shores of your old world.

Staying the Course

As part of your preparation for this journey, you put together a list of people you thought would be willing and able to support you as you make this transition. Now that you have gotten further into your transition, you probably have a better sense of where you need support and what kinds of specific support will help you stay the course and reach your destination.

Review your list of support people and think about who could help you in the areas that trouble you. Who would be good at providing emotional support? Who would be a good motivator? Who would have access to resources? The people on your list all care about your future and want you to succeed. All you have to do is ask for their help.

The three keys to effective use of a support system are

1. Knowing what you need.

2. Asking for what you need.

3. Realizing that you can't rely on one or two people to provide the full range of support that you will need.

As you become more skilled at recognizing your own needs, it will be easier for you identify which person to ask for the right kind of support.

WORKING WITH PROFESSIONAL COUNSELORS

You may also want to consider hiring a professional to facilitate your transition. Depending on your particular needs, you could choose to work with either a life coach or a career counselor. These are professionals trained to help you clarify your career goals, create and implement action plans, and develop new practices and behaviors. They are also prepared to provide the support, resources, and accountability that will ensure that you reach your stated goal.

If you decide to work with any professional, it is a good idea to interview at least three candidates so that you can find the best fit for you. Think carefully about what you are looking for in a coach/counselor. Write out a list of questions to ask so that you will be sure to get all the information you need. You'll probably want to know about each candidate's training and experience, whether they have a particular methodology, and the kinds of success they have had with clients. You also need to pay attention to how you feel when you are talking to each coach. Do you feel like you connect? Does you share a similar sense of humor? Do you feel that one understands you better than the others?

These are the intangible qualities that can make the real difference in a relationship. Not all professionals will offer you a good fit. To ensure the success of your coaching experience, you need to make sure that you choose the person you feel most comfortable with.

FINDING LIKE-MINDED ALLIES

Sometimes the people who can be the most supportive are people who have similar goals or who are going through a similar experience. So, you may discover that you can find a lot of support by attending workshops, seminars, or classes pertaining to your particular field of interest. If you want to find out more about the financial services field, attending an introductory seminar would not only give you the information you need, but it would also allow you to meet other people thinking about transitioning to the same field. Or if you are starting your own business and want to learn more about marketing, taking a marketing class for small businesses would introduce you to marketing ideas and other people starting up businesses.

There are a great many people and places that you can turn to for the help, support, and resources you need to keep moving forward. However, they rarely seek you out. It will be up to you to continuously monitor your needs and actively pursue the support you need. Sometimes asking for help can be difficult. You may believe asking for help is a sign of weakness. You may believe that asking for something you want is selfish. Or you may believe that people won't want to help you.

It is time to challenge those beliefs. Transitioning to a new career takes a lot of work, a lot of energy, and a great deal of support. Ask for the support you need. Don't let yourself fall short because of some outdated and inaccurate beliefs. You deserve to reach your dream.

The Light at the End of the Tunnel

The irony of any transition is that just as you are getting used to the uncertainty of navigating your way through the fog, the fog begins to lift and you can see where you are going. All the data you have gathered, all the informational interviews you have conducted, and all the networking you have done starts to come together. You are clear about the skills you want to use. You know what you value and need in a work environment. You know what interests you want to pursue and what competencies you want to develop. You have researched different fields of interest and talked to people in each area. You have stayed the course and your new career is beginning to take form.

Now as you near your destination, all you have left to do is make some final decisions about the field you are interested in working in and the specific type of position you are looking for. When you have decided on that, then it is just a matter of developing your resume and beginning the interviewing process. Yet, sometimes stepping into these final decisions can be difficult.

Making a definitive decision about your career is openly committing to a new professional path. You are putting your dreams and hopes out there for all to see and hear, and that takes courage. Your ideas are no longer just ideas. You goals are no longer goals. They are becoming reality and you are about to begin the next phase of your professional life. This is both exciting and frightening, and you should expect to see some of your old fears and uncertainties beginning to resurface.

If you find that you are beginning to doubt yourself, or if you are feeling a little uncertain about your decision-making abilities, take some time to review all of the steps you have taken to get this far. As you look at all the work you have done and all that you have learned during this journey, you will likely realize that you really are clear about the professional path you want to pursue. These current feelings of doubt and uncertainty are just your system's last-ditch attempts to get you to give up and allow it to return to normal.

CHECK IN WITH YOURSELF

If you really are having a difficult time making this decision, it is important that you identify what is getting in your way. It could be that you don't feel like you have enough information to be comfortable making a decision. This may or may not be true, and it is useful to check out the validity of your belief. It can be very easy to use the excuse of needing to gather more data as a diversionary tactic to keep you from having to actually make a decision.

One way to check out your assumption is to make a list of the information you feel you need and notice what kinds of things you are listing. Are you looking for specific pieces of data, or is your list filled with more general questions? If you truly need more information, take the time to get it. But if you are just distracting yourself by gathering superfluous data, the next step would be to figure out what fear or concern is causing you to avoid taking the next steps.

Another concern that can hold you back from decision making is the fear that you will make the wrong one. What if you choose a career that you end up hating? This could happen; but if you have done your homework, gathered information, talked with people, and spent time seriously thinking about the professional path that would fit you best, the likelihood of ending up in a horrible situation is small.

You also may be afraid that other people will think you are making the wrong decision. What if you want to move from a high-level position in the corporate world to starting your own landscaping business? In your heart, you know it's the right path, but you also know you are going to get a lot of questions and resistance from friends and family. It will take a lot to stand up to the pressure, and you can start to doubt yourself. This is when you will need to turn inward and listen to what you know is true for you and block out the voices of doubt that are bombarding you from the outside world.

Sometimes people are uncomfortable making a decision because they feel that once that decision is made, they have closed the doors to all other options. Their fear isn't about making the wrong choice. Their dilemma is the overwhelming selection of so many appealing possibilities.

If you find yourself experiencing this kind of indecision, the best thing to do is to give yourself a specific time frame in which to make your decision. Once it is made, do your best not to second-guess yourself or think about all the options you weren't able to choose. Keep your focus and energy on the choice you did make. If you truly can't make a decision, put three options in a hat and then pick one out. Since the issue here is not which one is right or wrong, you won't make a bad decision, but you will have made a decision and that will get you over the hump.

And the last of the common roadblocks to effective decision making is hoping that someone else will make the decision for you. You can make this happen by waiting too long to apply for a job and letting the application process close before you get your resume in. Your decision about that job has just been made for you. Or maybe someone in your old company gives you a call and says they have an opening in your old department and they would love for you to come back. You jump at the chance, not because you want to go back, but because someone has just taken away your need to make a real decision.

But what if your decision does not turn out the way you had hoped? What if you really do make a mistake? If this happens you have two choices. One is that you can view the situation as a failure and think of yourself as an incompetent decision-maker. Or you can use the situation as a learning experience, becoming aware of where you got tripped up so that it won't happen again. Making mistakes is how you learn and move forward in your life. Deciding not to step out and try new things is a good way to avoid failure. However, it is also a very good way to avoid success.

The journey of all transitions ends with a new beginning. As you make your final decisions regarding your next career, you are letting go of your old way of being and stepping into a new profession and a new way of being. And with this new beginning your current career transition comes to an end.

Creative
Career Changes

Popular Second Careers

Real People Profiles

Popular Second Careers

To love what you do and feel that it matters—how could anything be more fun?
        —Katherine Graham

This chapter will help you begin connecting the dots between the skills you have, the job characteristics you want, and possible career choices. The list of careers included in this chapter is by no means complete. It is only a starting point and is meant to act as a catalyst to jumpstart your own creative thought process.

The following sections describe some popular choices for second careers. As you read each description, keep your mind open and engage your creative thinking skills. Although the career described may not be what you are looking for, it may stimulate some ideas for other possibilities that you may want to pursue.

EVENT PLANNING

Event planning involves overseeing the details of an event to make sure it happens on schedule and within budget and that it is a success. Events can range from birthday parties to weddings, from conferences to fundraisers, from festivals to grand openings. If you like planning parties and find that your friends and family often call on you to help them put together special occasions, you may consider a career as an event planner.

This is a wide-open career field that has numerous advantages, including the following:

- Having the choice of working for yourself or an organization

- Being able to start small and learn as your business develops

- Having constant opportunity to use your creative skills

- Daily variety

- Work full- or part-time

- Potential for high earnings

- Getting paid for what you love to do

- Bringing joy to other people's lives

Skills and Knowledge Needed

Successful event planners are creative by nature, but they also need to have strong inter-personal and organizational skills. They must respect their clients and value the importance of providing excellent customer service.

In order to produce an event, planners work with many different types of people. These can include caterers, florists, hotel managers, and photographers. Each of these people has different needs and concerns. Planners need to be able to effectively communicate with each person involved to ensure the overall success of the event.

Planners also must have good organizational and time management skills. They are constantly juggling several tasks at once and coordinating the many details of each event. These include being in constant communications with the customer and vendors, preparation and follow-through on all contracts, and tending to any and all emergencies that arise. Being able to successfully pull all these parts together is what makes the difference between an okay event and a great event.

Personal Traits

People who enjoy this type of work are very creative individuals who derive great satisfaction from putting on magnificent events. They are outgoing, energetic self-starters who enjoy being around people. They don't get discouraged easily, get energized by multitasking, and love finding solutions to any problems that arise. They are resourceful and imaginative and delight in coming up with new and inventive ways for producing parties and events.

Obstacles and Disadvantages

The obstacles that event planners encounter depend on how they structure their business. If they are working for themselves, there are the issues of getting their own business up and running. These include building a client base, developing a broad base of reliable vendors, drafting client and vendor contracts, and general marketing of their business.

If they are working for an organization, the disadvantages can include working long hours, having too many events on their plate, and not having full creative freedom in planning the events.

Both private and corporate event planners devote many evening and weekend hours to work, as that is when the majority of events occur.

Professional Requirements

There is no special training or certifications needed to become an event planner. However, there are several training programs, online courses, and books available for people who want to learn more about this career or want information on how to develop their own event-planning business.

FINANCIAL PLANNING

Financial planning is the process of helping individuals meet their life goals through strategic management of their financial resources. If you are drawn to business and finance, if you enjoy coming up with creative solutions to problems, and you want to help people plan their financial future, you may consider a career in financial planning.

Advantages of working as a financial planner include the following:

*   Being your own boss
*   Flexible schedule

- High earning potential

- Intellectual stimulation and variety of daily tasks

- Ability to choose your work environment

- Fast-growing profession with room for growth

- Access to a wide variety of professional training and workshops

- Ability to make a difference in people's lives

Skills and Knowledge Needed

Financial planning requires a blend of different kinds of skills.

On the business side, planners need a strong understanding of the financial world. They have to be able to analyze and synthesize a wide spectrum of information. And because of the large amount of paperwork involved with each transaction, it is important that planners are highly organized and are good at attending to detail. New information is constantly coming out regarding taxes, insurance, retirement planning, and so on, and planners are responsible for keeping up with all the changes.

But planners also need good interpersonal skills. They are talking with people about their money, which can be a very emotional subject. Therefore, planners need to be able to listen and be understanding of their client's concerns, while providing them with accurate information and recommendations regarding their financial future. This can sometimes be a very thin line to walk.

Personal Traits

Successful financial planners are energized by the world of finance and find personal satisfaction in helping people achieve their financial goals. They are highly motivated people who enjoy being intellectually challenged and are excited by finding creative solutions to tough financial problems. They are entrepreneurs who are not afraid to take risks to ensure the success of their own business. They are self-starters who don't mind hard work and who will persevere in the face of difficulties.

Obstacles and Disadvantages

Financial planning is a career that has a lot of upsides to it, but it also has its share of obstacles and disadvantages. Some of these obstacles are inherent in starting any business, while others are specific to the financial planning field:

- High start-up costs: office space, computers, training, and a percentage of gross income goes to the parent company for administrative costs if you're opening a franchise

- Having to creating your own client base

- Steep learning curve; information regarding finance, estate, tax, and retirement planning is complex and constantly changing

- Uneven cash flow

- Highly competitive field

- Dealing with an emotionally charged issue—money

- Extensive paperwork

- Highly regulated field

Professional Requirements

The field of financial planning is regulated by the Securities and Exchange Commission. To be a financial advisor, you need to pass exams for federal and state licenses and registrations for securities, including the following:

- Series 7

- Series 63 or 66

- State life, accident, and health insurance

The Certified Financial Planner certification was created in 1972 to meet the professional development needs of those seeking to become financial planners. The CFP certification helps to distinguish those serious about a career in financial planning. Certification requirements include initial and ongoing education, examination, experience, and ethics components.

LIFE COACHING

Life coaches help people make the changes they want to make to strengthen competencies and enhance the quality of their lives. Coaching is about breaking through old barriers, noticing where the client's breakdowns occur, and helping them develop new practices and behaviors that will allow them to achieve their goals. If you are insightful, have a broad base of life experiences, and enjoy motivating and encouraging people, coaching may be a career for you to consider.

Advantages to being a life coach include the following:

- Being your own boss

- Having a flexible work schedule

- Being able to work from home

- Lots of opportunity for growth, since it's a relatively new field

- Being able to create your niche and work with the people/issues you want

- Opportunities to be creative in developing your own coaching strategies, programs, and resources

- Ongoing opportunities to integrate your life experience, both personal and professional, into your work

- Continuous opportunity for your own personal development

- Experiencing the satisfaction of making a positive difference in a person's life

Skills and Knowledge Needed

Coaching requires a blend of strong communication skills, powerful insight, and a good understanding of human beings. By listening, people can be helped to overcome their fears, can be offered complete objectivity, and be given undivided attention and unparalleled support.

Good coaches have the ability to interpret and frame information for the client in a manner that encourages that client to explore what is going on for them. Coaching uses communication, not to give clients the answers, but to help clients find the answers for themselves.

Coaches must be able to motivate and inspire people. They need to recognize the individual differences of their clients and tailor their coaching to these differences. Coaches also need the rigor to hold clients accountable for what they want to achieve. It is up to the coach to accurately assess clients' needs and know when their own professional skills are not adequate to address those needs. It is also the responsibility of the coach to have a strong network of outside resources they feel comfortable referring clients to, if needed.

Personal Traits

Successful coaches enjoy working with people. They are insightful and thorough listeners who know how to set and maintain clear boundaries. They are nonjudgmental and respectful of individual differences. They see potential in people and are comfortable stepping outside the box and using creative solutions to help clients reach their goals. Good coaches are dedicated and courageous people who are committed to their own ongoing personal and professional development and who are excited by the prospect of helping clients make positive and rewarding change in their lives.

Obstacles or Disadvantages

Many people enter the coaching profession with their focus solely on helping people make positive changes in their lives. They forget that coaching is a business and that starting and running a successful business takes a different set of skills from coaching clients. This is where many life coaches run into problems.

Often, coaches do not have the business experience or information needed to develop and run their practice. Many coaching schools do not offer classes in the business aspects of the profession, so it is up to the coaches to find the information and resources they need.

Because coaches are people-oriented, the business aspects of the profession can be uncomfortable for them. They want to spend their time helping their clients and may not enjoy marketing and networking or having to set and collect coaching fees. This can make it challenging to market and sell coaching services. And it is important to remember that coaching is a discretionary activity, so it is subject to fluctuations in the economy.

Additionally, many coaches work from home and this is often very isolating. Coaches need to be disciplined about creating networks for both personal and professional support.

Professional Requirements

Although coaching is a fairly new profession, there are coach training programs worldwide. Each school has its own coaching model and most have their own certification process. Some of these schools are accredited and some are not. At this point, the official accrediting body is the International Coach Federation. To learn more about coaching schools and certification, visit www.internationalcoachfederation.com or Peer Resources at www.peer.ca/coaching.html.

NONPROFIT WORK

A nonprofit is a tax-exempt organization that serves the public interest. In very general terms, the primary purpose of any nonprofit organization is to advocate, pursue, or advance a specific cause. Nonprofits span the spectrum of causes from human services to education, from the arts to politics, from religion to health care. If you want to make a difference in the world, don't care about getting rich, and enjoy working with like-minded people, you may want to consider a nonprofit career.

The many advantages to working in a nonprofit organization include the following:

- Working for a cause that is important to you

- Knowing that what you are doing will make a difference

- Sharing a common cause with your colleagues.

- Having variety in your daily activities

- Opportunities to take on different roles and different responsibilities

- More casual environment

Skills and Knowledge Needed

There are no unique business and organizational skills needed to work in nonprofits. Many of the skills that you have developed in the private sector can be transferred to nonprofit work.

But nonprofit work does require strong interpersonal and communication skills. Because nonprofits serve the public, there are many opportunities for staff to meet with the community. Being comfortable interacting with different groups of people and being able to clearly articulate the needs and accomplishments of the organization are important attributes for a nonprofit worker.

It is also important to be able to manage a variety of daily tasks. It is not unusual in nonprofits, especially the smaller ones, for staff to be responsible for more than one program. Staff members should be adaptable to changing routines, willing to take on new tasks, and resourceful so they can solve problems as they arise.

Personal Traits

People who work in nonprofits care more about making a difference in the world than they do about making money. They are idealistic individuals who enjoy the camaraderie of working with like-minded people. They feel passionate about the mission of the organization and are excited to have the opportunity to work on something they love. They are willing to take on a variety of tasks and responsibilities to help the organization be successful. They are creative, resourceful, and caring people who are energized by the impact of their work on the world.

Obstacles and Disadvantages

Working in a organization that is making a difference in the world is a special experience, but there are some disadvantages to nonprofit work. The first of these is the compensation. Although nonprofits are getting more competitive in their salary and benefit packages, many of them, particularly the smaller organizations, do not have the financial capacity to compete with the private sector.

Those who work in nonprofits also need to be cautious of burnout. Often, the populations they serve are high-need and that can take am emotional toll on the worker. Also, many organizations expect their staff members to take on multiple responsibilities. Because staff care so much about the mission of the agency, it can be hard for them to say no, thus leaving them with way too much on their plate.

One major frustration of working in nonprofits is the lack of funding. Much of their funding is soft money, which means that it is not guaranteed year to year. Therefore, agencies often find themselves in the position to have to cut programs and staff. As a result, nonprofits are constantly working to raise money to ensure the continuity of their programs and this never-ending quest for program dollars can take its toll on the staff.

Professional Requirements

Professional requirements such as special degrees and certifications would depend on the licensing requirements of your specific position. For more information about non-profit careers, visit www.idealist.org.

REAL ESTATE SALES

One of the most complex and important financial events in peoples' lives is the purchase or sale of a home or investment property. Because of this complexity and importance, people usually seek the help of real estate brokers and agents when buying or selling real estate. If you enjoy working with people, like selling (or think you would be good at it), like autonomy, and want to increase your earning potential, you may want to consider a career in real estate.

Some of the advantages of working in real estate include the following:

- Being your own boss

- The flexibility and freedom to set your own schedule

- Great potential for high earnings

- Opportunity for continued professional growth

- Constant variety in your daily tasks

- Opportunities to use both your intellectual and creative talents

- Satisfaction that comes from helping people find the house of their dreams

Skills and Knowledge Needed

Real estate requires a unique combination of business and people skills.

Agents need to be good at sales and marketing. Since they are their own bosses, it is important to have strong organizational and time management skills. And because of the ever-changing real estate market, they need to be comfortable doing research and analyzing data concerning market and business trends.

But business is only half of the real estate equation. Real estate is all about buying, selling, and getting people what they want. To do this successfully, agents need strong communication skills. Each relationship and every transaction requires the agent to draw on his or her listening, negotiating, conflict resolution, and creative problem-solving skills.

Personal Traits

Successful real estate agents are friendly, outgoing, and enjoy working with people. They are self-starters who are not afraid to take risks. They are responsible and able to respond to their clients' needs quickly and effectively. They like the challenge of starting and running a business and they take great pride in successfully completing each transaction. They are able to persevere in spite of difficulties and they get their energy from working with their clients and helping them successfully navigate the complex and often emotional roller coaster ride of buying or selling their homes.

Obstacles or Disadvantages

Although there are many benefits to working in real estate, there are also some drawbacks. For one, new agents are responsible for building their own client base. This is a slow process that involves soliciting friends and family, networking, and cold-calling. It can be both frustrating and discouraging.

Second, real estate professionals often struggle with and uneven flow of income. Since agents are paid when they close a transaction, there can be long stretches between paychecks. The uncertainty of a sporadic income can be emotionally draining, as well as cause problems with monthly budgeting.

And though agents have the flexibility of setting their own schedule, they do need to be available to show houses and meet with clients when it is convenient for the clients. As a result, much of their work is done on evenings and weekends.

Finally, there is a great deal of information that agents need to know regarding real estate law, transactions, taxes, and so on. This information is constantly being updated and it can be difficult to keep up with all the revisions.

Professional Requirements

Entry into the real estate profession takes preparation. Licensing is required, but specific requirements vary from state to state. In addition to 30 to 90 hours of classroom training, all prospective salespeople and brokers must pass a written exam. For more information on licensing, check with the Real Estate License Commission in your state.

REAL ESTATE STAGING

Real estate staging is the process of preparing any home for sale by making the home more visually appealing to the buyer. Stagers help set the stage to get homes sold more quickly and for more money. This is a relatively new career field and would be a great second career choice for anyone who has loves to redecorate, has an interest in interior design, and who would like to be his or her own boss.

Some advantages of working in this field include the following:

- Being your own boss

- Having a flexible work schedule

- Ability to work full- or part-time

- Relatively high profit margin

- Being a new field, there is a lot of opportunity for growth

- The opportunity to get paid for doing something you love

Skills and Knowledge Needed

Contrary to what you may believe, you do not have to have previous training in interior design to go into this field. There are several good programs available that offer courses in interior design and staging strategies to help develop and enhance your creative skills.

However, stagers need to have some basic business skills. They need to be comfortable marketing and networking their business. They need to be good at multi-tasking as they are likely to be handling several projects as once. They also need to have some management skills as they are likely to be overseeing moving crews in each of their projects.

Stagers also need to able to communicate effectively with their clients so that they will know what to expect and feel comfortable turning their homes over to the stager. Selling a home can be an emotional experience, and it is important for the stager to be able to put people at ease and engender a sense of confidence and trust as they work in people's homes.

Personal Traits

Successful stagers are outgoing, personable, and creative people who love making homes look more beautiful. They have the entrepreneurial spirit and are not afraid to step outside the box and take risks. They are self-starters who work well independently, but also enjoy working with other people. They are responsible and responsive to their clients. They see possibilities where others may see obstacles and they are good at finding creative solutions to any problems that may arise.

Obstacles or Disadvantages

Starting your own business always has its obstacles. As a stager, some of the common obstacles include the following:

- Creating your client base

- Uneven income flow

- Logistics of moving furniture in and out of homes

- Working under strict time constraints

- Dealing with the emotions of people trying to sell their homes

- Spending more time on creative aspects of job, and not tending to business details

Professional Requirements

As this is a fairly new profession there are no licensing or certification requirements. There are, however, certificate programs and special training programs to help people develop and enhance their interior design skills, and learn how to effectively start and run an interior redesign/staging business. For more information, visit the International Association of Home Staging Professionals at www.iahsp.com or the Interior Redesign Specialists at www.weredesign.com.

TEACHING

Teaching is growing faster than many other professions due to the large number of baby boomers who are retiring. If you have a specific area of knowledge or certain expertise that you really love, and if you get excited about the prospect of sharing your knowledge with other people, you may think about a career in teaching. Depending on your educational background, professional experience, and your area of interest, you may consider teaching at the secondary, community college, or university level.

The advantages to a career in education include the following:

- Flexible hours

- Opportunity to integrate your passion with your profession

- Opportunity to share your knowledge and love of a subject with others

- Possibility of conducting research in your subject area

- Future possibilities for further writing and speaking engagements

- Schedule flexibility may permit you to combine part-time teaching with other career paths

Skills and Knowledge Needed

Besides having extensive knowledge in their specific subject area, successful teachers need strong organizational and communication skills. They are responsible for planning their courses, execution of daily lesson plans, grading assignments, and meeting with students and other faculty. They have to be able to effectively prioritize their work and multitask to ensure that they successfully fulfill all their classroom responsibilities.

Good teaching is about engaging students in the learning process, and that requires strong communication skills. Successful teachers have the ability to draw their students in, making them active participants in the educational process through the use of thoughtful questions, reflective responses, dynamic group discussions, and diverse learning strategies.

Personal Traits

Good teachers are passionate about the learning process and a strong desire to pursue and disseminate knowledge. They are naturally curious, creative, and have the ability to motivate students through the use of multiple teaching strategies. Teachers need to be self-motivated, for they often work in environments with little direct supervision. They gain their energy from their love of learning and their ability to engage and motivate students.

Obstacles or Disadvantages

Teaching is a slightly different profession from many others in that people who choose this career path do so because they love learning and sharing their knowledge with others. Teaching is something you do because you are truly passionate about it.

Looking at teaching from that perspective, there are very few disadvantages. The one big issue that does come up is compensation. Although salaries vary depending on level of school, state, educational degrees, and experience, it is safe to say that teaching is not known for its high pay.

Other disadvantages include lack of tenure in many secondary education situations, which causes teachers to wonder each year whether their contract will be renewed, and lack of funding, which raises uncertainty about the future of programs and teaching positions each year.

Professional Requirements

Professional requirements will vary depending on the individual state and institution. Secondary education positions often times require a state teaching certificate. Community colleges require a master's degree or PhD, and for the most part all universities require a PhD. But these requirements may be waived if you have extensive experience or expertise in an area in high demand.

Real People Profiles

The following Real People Profiles are stories of ordinary people who took extraordinary leaps of faith in hopes of finding more satisfying and rewarding careers. As you will discover, they all had their share of doubts and uncertainty. They all ran into obstacles and experienced breakdowns. But each one believed enough in their dreams to stay the course and find a new career path that was better aligned with who they are and what they value in their lives. May their stories provide inspiration and motivation to you as you continue your journey to a new and more fulfilling career.

FROM METEOROLOGIST TO FINANCIAL ADVISOR

Name: Jeff
Previous career: meteorologist
Years in previous career: 11
Current career: financial advisor
Years in current career: 7
Personal status at time of transition: 34 years old; married

Tell me a little about your career as a meteorologist.

I wanted to be meteorologist since I was 10 years old. I went to college and majored in atmospheric sciences; when I graduated I was hired as a customized weather forecaster in the private sector. I was in that position for 11 years.

My job was to provide the detailed weather forecasts that our clients needed to best do their jobs. For example, road crews would need to know exactly when it was going to rain and how long it would last so that they could decide whether or not to go ahead with their paving. Energy companies needed to have an accurate long-range forecast so that they would know how much energy to import for a specified period of time.

What caused you to change careers?

There were several reasons that I decided to change careers. One reason was that there was really no place for me to move in my current position. I was second in command and my boss worked about 80 hours a week. My only logical move would be to take his position when he left, and knew I didn't want to work that much. I was also starting to get bored with the job. I communicated with my clients mostly by phone or e-mail. There was very little opportunity for building any kind of real relationships with them and I realized that I missed that.

I started doing some outside reading on business and found that I was fascinated by the area of finance. I continued my self-study and after a while my family and friends started coming to me with financial questions. I enjoyed working with them and I felt I was able to give them good advice. Then my company approached me and asked if I would set up their retirement plan. I had always thought that meteorology was my one passion, but I was seeing that I had another passion—finances. This started me thinking about possibly changing careers.

It might have taken me longer to make the leap and change careers, but there was a triggering event at work that helped me make up my mind. One day I had forecasted drizzle the entire morning. A construction crew needed to do some work and the foreman began calling me at 5:30 a.m. to see when the drizzle would stop. I told him it would last throughout the morning. He continued to call every hour getting more irate with each call. Finally about 9:00 a.m. he lost it and starting calling me every name in the book because it was still drizzling. It was at that point that I decided that I no longer needed this kind of aggravation and decided to change careers.

How did you decide what you wanted to do next?

Although I had a strong interest in finance, I also was curious about the real estate field. So, I did some research and talked to some real estate agents to get more information. It became quickly apparent that real estate would not be a good fit for me because

I didn't want to work on the weekends and be on call all the time. So, I shifted my focus to financial planning.

One of my co-workers had a financial advisor he really liked and he thought it would be useful for me to talk with her. So, I called her and scheduled an informational interview, which turned out to be incredibly helpful. The advisor talked about the good points and the not-so-good points of being a financial advisor and discussed the pros and cons of going out on my own versus working for a company. She was very open and willing to answer all the questions that I had about being an advisor.

I left the interview feeling that I had found my next career. Becoming a financial advisor would allow me to integrate my strong business skills, my need to keep learning, and my passion for finance with my desire to have a more flexible schedule and create long-term relationships with clients. It was the perfect combination for me.

How long did the actual transition take?

It took me a month to decide to leave my current job and 7 months to implement my transition plan.

What obstacles or breakdowns did you experience along the way?

Although it didn't take me too long to make this transition, there were several obstacles that I needed to overcome to make it happen. The first obstacle was convincing my wife that this was a good move for us. There was some anxiety on both our parts about trading a steady income for a variable income. There was a lot of training I had to go through and several industry tests that I had to pass before I could actually start working. And there was the financial cost of starting my own business. I had to make sure that I had enough money in reserve to not only cover the start-up costs, but also cover our living expenses as we got used to living on a variable income.

But the biggest obstacle was convincing the people at the company I chose to work with that I could make the transition from being a successful meteorologist to a successful financial advisor. The first hurdle I had to deal with was that I flunked the personality test that the financial company gave me to determine whether I would be a good financial advisor. The test didn't tell them why I wouldn't be good, just that I wasn't a good fit.

I knew I could be very good at this, and I wasn't going to let some test get in my way. After several calls I convinced them to let me come in for the introductory interview. I received a very high score on the basic interview so I was invited to come back for a real job interview. Their main question still was why I would be good at this. I had to come up with some way to clearly show them that the skills I used as a meteorologist were transferable.

I first told them about my passion for finance and how I much I had learned through my self-study program. I told them about the retirement plan I had set up for my company.

I then told them about working with my clients and how the decisions they made based on my weather predictions were financial decisions. The clients had projects that had to get done, but they couldn't afford to spend their money foolishly. It was up to me to help them walk that thin line between risk and reward.

Although my arguments were somewhat compelling, I think it was my obvious passion for the field and belief in myself that finally won them over. I knew I would make a great financial advisor; I just had to make them see that. And finally, they did. I worked as a financial planner for the company for 2 years. After I successfully completed their training programs and reaching a certain level of production, I was given the opportunity to take my clients and create my own franchise branch.

What did you learn about yourself as you went through this process?

I became much clearer about what I needed in a work environment. I found out how important interpersonal relationships are to me. I realized that I enjoy the flexibility of working for myself. I like being able to take a day off when I want and I like the fact that if I work hard, my income reflects my effort.

I also learned that it is really important to reach for what I want and to not let fear and doubt get in my way. There were some tough times as I worked to get my business established. It was hard to find clients and my paychecks were sometimes very small. But I loved what I was doing. I knew in my heart I was doing the right thing and I just had to trust that it would work out.

What advice would you give people thinking about a career change?

The most important thing to me is to make sure you are going towards something you love. Don't change careers just because you think the grass might be greener somewhere else. Identify what you love to do and then go for it. Make sure that you take time to prepare for the change. Look at your finances and make sure you and your partner are both in agreement about the change. Then make the transition and don't look back.

Do you feel you are in the right career for you at this point?

Yes, without a doubt. I get up every morning excited to go to work. I am constantly learning new things and expanding my skills as an advisor. I have developed wonderful relationships with my clients, and I feel really good about being able to help them secure their financial future. I feel very lucky to be in a job I like so much.

FROM JUVENILE JUSTICE ADVOCATE
TO HIGH-TECH DIRECTOR

Name: Barbara

Previous career: coordinator for juvenile detention ministry

Years in previous career: 4

Current career: senior director at a large computer manufacturer

Years in current career: 10

Personal status at time of transition: 26 years old; single

Tell me a little about your career as a juvenile justice advocate.

I was doing advocacy work for kids in prison and jails. My job included direct counseling, identifying community support resources, and helping to educate communities about the needs of youth coming through the juvenile justice system. I was making about $6 an hour doing work that involved in-court translation, community public speaking, and helping suicidal kids sort through their lives and identify options. It seemed like important work for me and I found it very fulfilling.

What caused you to change careers?

During my fourth year in this job I realized I needed to make more money in order not to go into serious debt. Then a series of unrelated, but almost simultaneous, events happened that caused me to seriously rethink my professional path. My rent doubled, my car was totaled, and my primary relationship fell apart leaving me with higher living expenses, complicated logistics, and a broken heart.

I took a few weeks off recuperate, and when I came back I realized that the situations at work that had previously been interesting and challenging now seemed overwhelming and emotionally draining. My emotional reserve was bordering on empty, and my expenses had grown higher than my income.

So, I began looking for what I thought of as an "oasis" while I got back on my feet. I was looking for a temporary career change that would reduce the emotional energy I had to expend and increase my income so that I could afford my life again.

How did you decide what you wanted to do next?

I used the network of people that I had around me to help me with my next step. In my job with the juvenile justice system I had taken on responsibility for publishing a newsletter using computer software, and I enjoyed the artistic side of that work.

One of the people I had met in my training program for the youth advocacy position came from a strong computer skills background, and she worked at a local software company that dealt with that publishing software. I decided to talk with her about what I should do and she encouraged me to interview for some temporary positions with her company.

It sounded good to me. The job sounded intellectually engaging, and I figured I'd make about $10 per hour, which would be a significant increase for me. My financial pressures would be eased and I could take some time to figure out my next career move.

By the time I was ready to apply, my friend had moved to another software company that was also hiring. So, in order to increase my probability of getting a job, I applied to both companies. Although I knew a little about the first company, I really knew nothing about the second.

The first company interviewed me for a temporary position. The interview lasted about 35 minutes; they thanked me for my time and didn't hire me because I had no formal computer knowledge or background, even though I was very fluent with their product.

The second company interviewed me for a full-time position (though at the time of the interview I thought it was a temporary position all the way through the process). The interview lasted about 4 hours and I spoke with six different people.

I had borrowed a book about computers the night before the interview and memorized 2 pages on "network printing on the Macintosh." I knew next to nothing about computers, had no idea what networks were, or for that matter whether the computer was in the monitor or in the box on the floor. But the topic had nice graphics and I just had the feeling that it might be important to know something about it.

As luck would have it, four of the six people I met with that day asked me to tell them what I knew about printing issues. So, with my 2-page memorized spiel about network printing, I used a skill I learned from college essays about rephrasing the question enough times in enough ways to make it seem that I was actually saying something meaningful. The fifth person found out that I worked with kids in trouble with the law and spent the 45 minutes asking me for advice about how to deal with her teenage daughter.

The sixth person was the HR manager. She looked at my resume, looked at the job description, and looked me in the eyes. She said, "It seems like you have absolutely zero background or knowledge about computers. And it looks like you've spent the last 4 years in jails and prisons. Can you help me understand why you applied for this position?"

So, I told her that if I could deescalate a suicidal, homicidal adolescent who was in a cell with a rival gang member whose mother had just gone into drug treatment, then I probably could handle a customer on the phone who was upset about her computer. And then I pointed out my exceptional grade point averages from high school and college. I told her that I was smart and could learn anything I needed to about computers, but that I didn't think that people who knew about computers could learn the skills I had in dealing with people who were angry.

She nodded thoughtfully, thanked me, and gave me no impression of what she was thinking. Two days later I received a full-time offer for $24,000 per year plus full benefits and a paid health club membership. This was 1990, and that figure was a higher salary at that time than I thought I would ever make in my adult life. And my life changed course.

How long did the actual transition take from decision to being hired?

About 2 months.

What obstacles or breakdowns did you experience along the way?

The first obstacle was my ignorance of the choices available to me. The second obstacle was my lack of formalized technical knowledge. But both of those obstacles were offset by my confidence in my own value as an employee and by my willingness to talk about my situation and ask for ideas and help.

By talking with different friends, I was able to broaden my own perspective about what I had to offer the software world. These supportive friends gave me the foundation to go into the situation and demonstrate confidence. The willingness of the hiring managers to take a risk on me paid off for them, for me, and for that company many times over. But it was a risk that we all took, because I didn't look like the type of person on paper that would be a natural fit in that job.

What did you learn about yourself as you went through this process?

I learned that persistence is invaluable. I also learned that it is important to be able to clearly articulate how my set of skills can be effectively transferred. Although it was easy for me to see, others didn't always have the same vision. And I learned that being honest and open with friends and allowing their insight to assist me in identifying choices makes my horizons boundless.

In hindsight, what would you have done differently?

I have to say that this particular transition was pretty smooth. I was supported in a steadfast manner by friends and colleagues and they carried me along emotionally and financially; they were my best resources until I could maintain my footing.

What advice would you give people thinking about a career change?

- Identify transferable skills.

- Understand what type of energy you have to give out.

- Think about whether the jobs you're looking at will provide you with the right level of challenge and require the type of energy that you have available.

- Talk to people who know you and know your skill set and ask them who/what they think you could do.

- Get some sort of professional level certification on your resume from a local community college or university extension program to show prospective employers that you have some sort of recent training in the area that you're interested in.

- Join a professional association that offers conferences and training in the area you're choosing and attend those conferences, volunteer with the association, and use the network.

- Ask for help.

- Send lots of people your resume just because. You never know where it will end up, but it will not end up anywhere if you don't send it out.

Do you feel you are in the right career for you at this point?

The software industry was a good fit for me. In the 10 years I've been here, I've had many interesting and diverse jobs. I received amazing on-the-job training, support for a master's degree, and the financial resources to make many other subsequent choices. I also had the opportunity to meet, work with, and learn from many incredible people who helped to support and challenge me by continually giving me interesting and complex problems to solve.

FROM CHEF TO CRITICAL CARE NURSE

Name: Michael
Previous career: chef
Years in previous career: 6
Current career: critical care nurse
Years in current career: 2
Personal status at time of transition: 32 years old; single

Tell me a little about your career as a chef.

I had originally wanted to become a nurse, so after I graduated from high school I attended a nursing orientation at a local community college. I talked with one of the instructors after the orientation and was given the impression that registered nurses were going to be eliminated from the hospital in order to save money. I thought there would be no work for me. I knew I loved to cook and create; so, I decided to go to culinary school and become a chef.

What caused you to change careers?

I remember lying in bed at 3:57 a.m. and groaning as my alarm clock went off for a third time. I had truly mastered the snooze button. I had to be downtown at work by 5:00 a.m. and still had a 40-minute commute ahead of me. I had enough time for a quick shower, but a coffee would have to wait. I was lucky; I found one chef coat and a pair of checkered pants in the dryer.

During the commute to work that morning, the radio was on some morning talk show, but I wasn't really listening. I starred blankly at the empty freeway in front of me and thought, "At least it's my Friday." I then wondered if there were people out there that didn't care that the weekend was approaching . . . or didn't hate Monday mornings.

During the past 2 months, I had been neglecting to keep professional edges on my knives. In fact, I remember using my 3-inch paring knife to open a can of Dijon. I no longer set out a clean pair of checkered pants and white chef's coat the night before work. Actually, I didn't even bother to separate the two in the laundry anymore, giving the chef's coat a subtle grey hue. Finally, I no longer looked foreword to work. My new goal was to spend the least amount of time there as possible.

Other cooks might say I couldn't hack the hard work. But I have a great work ethic. I simply didn't enjoy what I was doing. After completing over 2 years of culinary arts school and practicing that art for another 2 years, I realized that this was not what I had hoped for. My food was not what it once was, my attitude was poor, and my drive to be better was almost completely depleted. I knew I had to make a decision before the career made it for me.

How did you decide what you wanted to do?

As I thought about a new career my mind wandered back to my love of nursing. When I was in the fourth grade I was retrieving a football out of a large fir tree. I was about 30 feet up when my foot slipped and I fell to the ground. I was seriously injured and during the next 3 years, I endured six surgeries. Although all the people involved—fire-fighters, paramedics, and doctors—did a great job, the people I remember most were the nurses.

They were always there to comfort me, to explain procedures to me, and to hold my hand. It was obvious that they truly cared about me, and their support and caring made a huge difference in my recovery. The role they played during those difficult years was pivotal in my life, and I knew that someday I wanted to be in a position to affect other people's lives in that same way.

As I thought about it more, nursing seemed like the right choice, but I decided to talk with a career counselor just to make sure. After talking with the counselor and taking a battery of aptitude and vocational tests, all the signs pointed me toward nursing.

During this transition time I was cooking for a local hospital, so I took that opportunity to talk with the nurses, respiratory therapists, and supporting hospital staff about their experiences during nursing school and in their career. The more information I gathered, the clearer it was that I wanted to go into nursing.

I made my final decision by remembering the values that I held near to my heart, such as helping others and the ability to grow within the field. I will always remember the impact that the emergency nurse made on me when she helped save my life in the fourth grade. Making that same kind of impact on other people's lives was very attractive to me.

How long did the actual transition take from decision to being hired?

The first part of the transition took about a year and a half. This time was spent taking the classes I needed just to apply to nursing school. Once I finished with the prerequisites, I applied and was accepted into nursing school, which was a 2-year program. After graduating from nursing school I had to pass the national board test for nursing licensure. I was lucky. I passed the boards on my first attempt and was invited immediately into an ICU residency program. So, the total time from deciding to change careers to actual paid employment was about 4 years, but it was well worth the time, energy, and money.

What obstacles or breakdowns did you experience along the way?

The G.P.A. requirements were fairly high when I was accepted into the nursing program and it was tough to know that I had to do well.

Another obstacle many students face is lack of money. I worked full time while completing my prerequisites and sacrificed a lot of sleep. When I was in nursing school, I worked part-time and took out as many loans that I could qualify for. Living poor while you are in school is tough and many people use that as an excuse to not go back to school—but you just have to remember that it's not forever.

What did you learn about yourself as you went through this process?

I used to hate the sciences and now I see it was only because I didn't understand them. My first quarter of anatomy and physiology (A&P) was utterly confusing. During the second quarter when I was taking A&P, microbiology, and one of the chemistry classes, they all made sense and were really very similar in nature.

I also found out that I love working with people and helping them get well. One of the trauma surgeons stopped by the ICU a few weeks ago just to let the nursing staff know how well one of the patients was doing. It was a patient we thought might not survive. That feeling is paramount on the list of reasons I became a critical care nurse.

In hindsight, what would you have done differently?

I feel the process went fairly smoothly. I camped out in the nursing office a lot of the time and I met nurses everywhere. I would make an effort to pick their brains, and nurses love to talk about what they do for a living. I guess the process went as well as it did for me because I attempted to gather as much information about nursing as possible. This allowed me to make an informed decision.

What advice would you give people thinking about a career change?

I would ask them to stop and think about what really makes them happy and then figure out what career will get them closest to that feeling. If you truly love what you are doing, then you will be successful.

Do you feel you are in the right career for you at this point?

I am definitely in the right career at this time. I love what I do and I think I would do this job for a much smaller wage. I now look forward to the work as opposed to looking forward to the weekends.

FROM RESEARCHER/INSTRUCTOR TO ENVIRONMENTAL EDUCATOR

Name: Shelly

Previous career: social researcher/college instructor

Years in Career: 10

New career: environmental educator

Years in new career: 1

Personal status at time of transition: 43 years old; married

Tell me a little about your career as a social researcher.

My initial work as a social researcher began when I was a graduate student working on my PhD. After completing my doctorate degree I worked in the research department of a nonprofit national organization that provided foster care and adoption services. My position provided program evaluation, technical support, and consultation to programs within and outside of the organization. I also taught part-time as a university instructor. I taught social research courses and adult development courses.

What caused you to change careers?

My work was no longer fulfilling for me, and I felt a lack of enthusiasm for what I was doing. I just felt stuck. For a long time I had a voice inside me telling me that I needed to do something that was more environmentally focused. That instead of just donating time and money to environmental organizations, I wanted to make it more of my professional work. I wasn't really sure what that would look like; so, for a long time I ignored it. Then an opportunity presented itself when I was laid off from my program evaluation position. This provided me an opening to pursue my interest in the environment. I continued to work as a university instructor but knew that I wanted something different.

How did you decide what you wanted to do next?

Although I have always been very interested in the environment, I didn't think it would be possible to make that transition. My training was in research and academic teaching. I didn't feel I had the skills, knowledge, or experience I needed to get any kind of job in the environmental field.

So, I began looking for jobs that were within my field. That seemed like the safe and sensible thing to do. However, after several months of not getting any job leads, I realized I was stuck. I had no energy for jobs in the world of academic research, and I didn't know what to do.

It was at this point that I decided to work with a career coach. It didn't take too long for my interest in the environment to resurface. I had been volunteering at the local aquarium and I knew in my heart that this was the right path for me. I was just getting stalled by lack of information of what was available and how my skills might transfer to this new field.

I began doing some research. Books and the Internet were great sources for gathering general data and seeing what jobs were available, but the most valuable information came from doing informational interviews. As I talked with people, I learned more about the opportunities that were open to me, and the more I learned the more excited I got. I discovered that there were many career opportunities available to me within this field. I just needed to decide which area would be the best fit for me.

I decided to take a couple of part-time positions to test the waters. Currently I am working for an education institute that is evaluating the impact of using environmental education tools in the classroom. I am also working part-time as an interpreter and supervisor at the local aquarium, and I am involved in a beach naturalist program. I am beginning to see that my passion lies with teaching, marine life, and conservation. I am planning to pursue these interests by taking some courses in marine biology and the environment.

How long did the actual transition take from decision to being hired?

Once I gave myself permission to investigate environment-related job opportunities, it took me 8 months to find a job. But it took me 2 years to give myself permission to look outside the box and explore a career path outside my field of expertise.

What obstacles or breakdowns did you experience along the way?

My biggest obstacle was not being financially prepared for a career transition. This caused me to have to work at too many jobs to make ends meet. At one point I was working four different part-time jobs, which left me completely exhausted. My life felt out of control. I didn't have the time or energy to do anything except go to work and go to sleep. When I got that tired, my perspective on things would get very narrow and I would begin doubting my ability to make this transition. I would lose sight of the big picture and what I wanted next.

What did you learn about yourself as you went through the process?

I learned that I could do informational interviews. I learned that people really do like talking about their jobs and being helpful to newcomers. Through these interviews I began to see that I did have a lot of useful skills and talents, which really helped to increase my confidence.

I also learned that I need structure and need to be accountable to someone if I am going to successfully navigate this kind of transition. If I were left on my own, I found myself easily veering off course and losing my focus and direction. Knowing that I would be talking to my coach every week motivated me to take action on things in a much more timely fashion.

In hindsight, what would you have done differently?

I wish I had been more financially prepared. The constant worrying about money was an unneeded stress, not to mention the effects of carrying four part-time jobs. I wish I had thought more about what the effects would be of transitioning into a new career area, such as taking entry-level positions (in order to gain experience and see where my interests lay) that do not pay as well as my teaching and evaluation work. The stress of not having enough money caused me at times to rush into taking jobs that, if I had had a financial cushion, I may not have taken.

I also could have been better organized throughout this process, although organization has never been my strong suit. I wasn't always as clear and intentional in the direction of my work as I would have liked, but maybe that is part of the learning and growing process.

One of the things that I really wish I had done was to build in more time for networking. For me, networking is one of the most effective strategies for meeting new people, gathering useful information, and opening doors to new possibilities. I had an effective networking schedule in place when I started this process, but as I got busier, my networking seemed to go by the wayside.

What advice would you give people thinking about a career change?

The first piece of advice I would give anyone is to do informational interviews. They are by far the best way to gain the kinds of information you need to make informed career decisions. It also helps to build up your confidence about the skills you have and how they can transfer to the areas you are interested in.

I would encourage people to take risks. As scary as this might sound, it is the only way to move your life ahead. Staying in the comfort of what is known to you will only keep you stuck. Take a chance and try something new even if it's not perfectly right. You will learn so much.

I would also tell people to make sure you get support as you go through this process. Work with a coach, counselor, or mentor, or pull together a network of friends that you can count on. This kind of life transition can be very trying and to attempt to do it alone just doesn't make sense. I learned that the hard way.

Do you feel you are in the right career for you at this point?

Although I don't feel this transition is completely over, I do know I am on the right career path. It is a great feeling to be working in a field that feeds my passion, that gives me constant opportunities for learning, and that allows me to use my knowledge and skills in teaching and research. With each new experience, I am gaining clarity about the path that lies ahead of me.

FROM SOCIAL SERVICES PROJECT MANAGER TO PUBLIC POLICY CONSULTANT

Name: Eric

Previous career: social services project manager

Years in previous career: 10

Current career: public policy consultant—private sector

Years in current position: 7

Personal status at time of transition: 40 years old; married

Tell me a little about your career as a social services project manager.

I was working for a university as a project manager for neighborhood intervention programs. These programs dealt with issues such as teen pregnancy, STDs, and drug abuse. The university secured the grant money and I managed the programs.

What caused you to change careers?

Although I loved what I was doing, being dependent on grant money for my job began to take its toll. I had always wanted to test the waters of the private sector, but I wasn't quite sure how to make that change. Then a game of basketball changed all that.

Every week I played pick-up basketball with a good friend of mine who was also looking to break into the business world. We both knew we had a lot of skills and that we could be getting paid a lot more money in the private sector. Each week after our game we would bounce ideas around trying to come up with creative ways to combine our skills and talents with our interests and passions in ways that would be more exciting and challenging for us.

Out of one of our brainstorming sessions, our first business idea was hatched. We decided to publish a small magazine that would rate the weekly pick-up basketball games that took place around the city. It would let people know what kinds of games were being played where on any given day of the week. So, whether you were a weekend jock or a NBA hopeful, you would be able to locate the game that would work best for you. We also planned on including articles on health, nutrition, and exercise.

We had a lot of energy behind this idea because of our passion for basketball; however, we knew nothing about the publishing business. But we were determined to make it work. We put together a business plan, pulled together a small group of investors and we were off and running.

This experience was the turning point in both of our lives. When we started we had no experience with copywriting, printing, advertising, interviewing, fundraising, etc. But since we didn't have a staff, we had to rely on ourselves to get things done. And through the process of getting this magazine up and running, we realized that we had all the skills necessary to be successful in the business world.

How did you decide on what you wanted to do next?

I had always wanted to work in the private sector, I just wasn't exactly sure what kind of position I wanted to pursue. One day I was talking with a friend of mine who worked for a large insurance company about my situation and he thought I should set up an informational interview at his company. So, with his encouragement, I scheduled an interview with the CEO and that conversation changed the course of my professional life.

During the interview, I proposed the idea of the company opening satellite offices in neighborhoods to create stronger links between the insurance company and the community. The CEO was interested enough to invite me to put together a formal proposal. This was very exciting, for not only was there the possibility of a great job in my future, but it would be a job that combined all the things I loved doing—community relations, program development, and creative problem solving.

The presentation went well. The company decided to go ahead with the idea and created their first community satellite office; I was hired to implement the development plan and to be the center's first director.

How long did the actual transition take from decision to being hired?

The actual transition took about 1 month.

What obstacles or breakdowns did you experience along the way?

The main obstacle I faced was getting the insurance company to see how important this center would be not only to the neighborhood that it would serve, but also the long-term benefits for them. I had to make sure that I created a proposal that would effectively address all the issues and questions that were likely to come up.

Another obstacle was my lack of knowledge about the insurance industry. Although the ultimate mission of the center revolved more around building community relationships than insurance issues, I needed to be able to talk about the center using language and concepts that insurance people could relate to. It took a lot of research and a great deal of creative thinking on my part to be able to translate my thoughts and ideas into "insurancese."

What did you learn about yourself as you went through this process?

I learned how important it was to me to be doing something that I really loved. I found out how much I enjoy being challenged and using my creative thinking skills. As I became more involved in developing the proposal, I could feel both my confidence and excitement growing and I knew that I was on the right career path.

There is a pervasive belief that it's not possible to transition from the social service world to the corporate world—that the skills and cultures are too different. Although I didn't fully buy into that belief, there was a part of me that questioned my ability to make it in the corporate environment. Going through this process erased all doubts that I had, and completely validated the trust and confidence I had in myself to be successful.

In hindsight, what would you have done differently?

This was an easy transition because I had the great fortune of creating and stepping into the perfect job for me.

What advice would you give people thinking about a career change?

The first thing I would tell them is to make sure they do what they really love doing. It can be very easy to settle for jobs because you know you can do them. But if there is no passion behind it, you will get bored very quickly. I would also tell them to step out of their comfort zone. There are unlimited possibilities out there but you will never find what you are looking for unless you venture into new territory.

I would also suggest that people test the waters of potential careers by volunteering or taking on projects within that field. Don't be afraid to put yourself out there and try new things. Every time you do something new, you gain new skills and you never know when you might need those skills.

The other piece of advice I would give people is to talk to friends and colleagues about what you are looking for. The more people you talk with, the more ideas you get and the more doors that open. It is also easy to for us to be critical of our own ideas, but bouncing them off other people can create a synergistic effect that can birth a great new idea. Our magazine was a great example of this kind of collaborative thinking.

But the most important thing to remember is to not sell yourself short, trust what your heart is telling you, and don't let anything stand between you and your dream.

Do you feel you are in the right career for you at this point in time?

Yes. I love my job. I get to do what I love doing and I get paid well for doing it. I am constantly being challenged to think outside the box and I thrive on that. The skills that I developed through my social work career have been a huge asset and have helped me achieve things I could have never done if I didn't have them. I love being given the opportunity to solve problems, connect people, and to make good things happen.

FROM TRUST OPERATIONS ASSOCIATE TO ENTREPRENEUR

Name: Joanne

Previous career: banking—trust operations associate

Years in previous career: 15

Current career: entrepreneur

Years in current career: 1

Personal status at time of transition: 52 years old; married

Tell me a little about your career in banking.

I was responsible for the daily trust operations of the bank. It was my responsibility to manage the accounting functions of all the trust clients, to answer any questions, and solve any problems that arose.

What caused you to change careers?

I found it very disheartening working in the corporate world. The emphasis was always on the bottom line. I became tired of working nine-to-five. I wanted more flexibility in my work schedule and I wanted more control over the money I made. I also wanted to feel like I was contributing something to the world and that what I did professionally, as well as personally, made a positive difference.

How did you decide what you wanted to do next?

I always knew I wanted to be an entrepreneur and run my own small business. I just wasn't quite sure what kind of business it would be. I did a lot of daydreaming about what it would mean to be an entrepreneur and watched what kinds of thoughts and ideas passed through my mind. I visited small businesses and paid attention to how I felt in different kinds of environments. I read books on career transitions. I attended seminars and workshops on starting your own business. I thought about the things I like to do as a child. And I made a list of the natural skills I had that I enjoyed using.

As I went through this process, two things became very clear. The first was that my heart has always been tied to my home. My home is where I get my energy. The second was that I really loved creating different types of home crafts. I had been making crafts my whole life and it seemed a natural next step to incorporate my hobby into my business.

As I thought about this more, I became very excited about the prospect of starting a small business that would combine a crafts store and a small café. I wanted to create a comfortable place for people to sit, talk, and hopefully buy a craft or two. Thus, my business, Something Simple, was born.

My craft business has a slightly different slant than most because I only use recycled or gently used materials in making my items. I also only make things that are usable in a home such as pillows, candles, coat racks, and quilts, for I believe that the world has enough knick-knacks.

How long did the actual transition take from decision to being hired?

After 6 months, my business is still a work in progress. Although I am making my crafts and selling them, I have yet to find the perfect spot for my café.

What obstacles or breakdowns did you experience along the way?

The biggest obstacle that I faced in this transition was fear. I have always worked for someone else and to step out on my own at this point in my life was very scary. In my heart I knew this is what I wanted to do, but sometimes the voice of doubt and uncertainty would drown out the voice in my heart. I did not grow up in a family of entrepreneurs so I didn't have any role models. What I was doing was very exciting, but sometimes it felt like I was stepping too far out of my comfort zone.

Being outside my comfort zone would not have been so hard if I were more comfortable asking for help or support. But I have always been very independent and believed that I have to do everything by myself. As a result, I don't avail myself of all resources that are available and end up having to reinvent the wheel, which takes both my time and energy.

Another obstacle was I didn't feel I had the adequate knowledge to run a small business. Although I have worked in the business world all my life, there was something about starting my own business that seemed to challenge my confidence.

What did you learn about yourself as you went through this process?

Going through this process reinforced how important it was for me to be able to integrate my values into all aspects of my life. One of the main reasons I was so unhappy in my banking job was that my work environment was counter to many of my core values.

I also became aware of just how much I enjoy working for myself. Even in the worst times when I would feel scared or uncertain about something in my business, I never thought about going back to work someone else. I love being my own boss

In hindsight, what would you have done differently?

I would have listened to my heart earlier. It took me 10 years to make the decision to leave. I knew I wasn't happy in my old job, but I would find ways to distract myself from my unhappiness. I would tell myself that I would "get over it" and that the job I had was a good job. I would try and appease myself by buying things I didn't need. That would only add to my financial debt and then I would think I had to stay in my job. I spent a lot of energy trying to convince myself not to listen to my heart.

The second thing I wish was that I had been more aware of the financial impact involved with this kind of transition. If I had gone into this process with a little greater financial stability, the transition would have probably been quicker and easier.

What advice would you give people thinking about a career change?

The first thing I would say is whatever your dream may be, go for it. I waited 10 years because I was waiting for everything to be just right in my life before I took the leap. I finally saw that there would always be reasons why it isn't the right time to change careers. You just need to do it.

Second, I would tell people to plan for the change, but don't get bogged down in the planning. This kind of transition does take some preparation, but once again, it can be easy to put off getting started because you don't feel you have done adequate planning. For me, that was just an excuse.

And most important, keep dreaming. Don't let the confines of everyday life keep you from imagining all the possibilities waiting for you out there. Dreams were what kept me going through all those years in the corporate world, and they are what sustains my business today.

Do you feel you are in the right career at this point in time?

There is no doubt that I am in the right career at this point in my life. I waited a long time to get here and I had plenty of time to think about what it was that I wanted to do. I am now doing exactly what I want to be doing and that is a very special feeling.

FROM INTERNATIONAL BUSINESS EXECUTIVE TO ENTREPRENEUR

Name: Cenmar

Previous career: international business executive

Years in previous career: 10

Current career: entrepreneur

Years in current career: 4

Personal status as time of transition: 36 years old; divorced; one child

Tell me a little about your previous career.

I was living and working in Tokyo as an executive for a Fortune 500 company.

What caused you to change careers?

There were three precipitating events that took place over a period of 3 months before my transition. The first was dissatisfaction with the leadership of my company. I had problems respecting the decisions being made by the top echelon. We had a CEO who seemed to lack a long-term vision for the organization. Rather than projecting strong leadership traits, he came across as shallow. His values and modus operandi were very different from mine. I began to ask myself if my work (and life) was making any meaningful impact in the lives of others. It was then that the answer to my own question, which was a loud "NO," hit me hard.

I had also met two very important people in my life while living in Japan. One of them was my Zen master. He is a truly enlightened human being. Our meetings began to shatter many of my long-held beliefs and assumptions.

The second important person in my life at this time was an entrepreneur. He was one of the world's wealthiest people. This man was much more than his wealth and business empire. His passion was transforming the way we live our lives. What I most admired about this man was the depth of his vision and understanding of human history. He had a powerful understanding of things to come, because he was an avid student of the past. He understood how individuals can play significant roles in the transformation of the societies they come from and beyond. For me, glimpsing the world from his perspective opened completely new possibilities. I understood that entrepreneurship was the art of making ideas work in the real word. At that time, I realized that it was much more interesting to be an entrepreneur that to be a corporate manager.

And third, as a divorced father of a 6-year-old girl, I realized that not seeing my daughter grow was too high a price to pay for any corporate career. She visited me with my mother in Tokyo for a couple of months. I spent as much time as I could manage with them, but at the end of that visit, I realized how much I was missing out on. After her departure, I began to feel that an important stage of my life was coming to an end. It was then, when I realized fully the main reasons my life had taken me across the Pacific, so far away from everyone and everything I knew.

How did you decide what you wanted to do next?

I knew I wanted to start my own business. I had done a lot of thinking about the potential of the Internet in providing business-to-business solutions, and I knew there was immense business opportunity available in this area. I also knew that, based on my international business background, I wanted to focus my efforts first in Latin America and then move in other markets.

The combination of my desire to build a vibrant, multidimensional organization and my desperation to return to the United States provided me with more than enough motivation to start moving immediately toward my dreams. I wrote a business plan and met with some Brazilian investors I knew. I was lucky to get the initial investment I needed, and in 1999 I founded Latin America's first Web-based business-to-business e-procurement solution.

How long did the actual transition take from decision to being hired?

I took about 6 months for me to write my business plan and to secure the seed investment.

What obstacles or breakdowns did you experience along the way?

My biggest challenge initially was beginning the execution of my new business venture, while still employed in my overseas assignment. "Moonlighting" was not that much fun and required many late-night conference calls and e-mails. Keeping things in order and moving forward required a good amount of creativity on my part. Also, early on I realized that my partners and I had very different communication styles. Mistakenly, I brushed this off as something that could be worked out easily as the venture progressed.

What did you learn about yourself as you went through this process?

I learned a lot. Our partnership eventually failed and the venture eventually closed four of its five international locations. However, the first 2 years were an incredible journey. We managed to raise over $15 million in private investment equity and built a team of 60 talented people in five countries. Our first year revenues exceeded $3 million and we had well-known firms such as Citibank, PepsiCo, and Nestlé as our clients.

While I learned a great deal about business during the whole process, the real lessons came with failure. After recovering from the initial shock and disappointment, I began to understand my own role in the events and to take responsibility for my contribution to the failure of the venture.

Most importantly, I realized that by starting an international business venture, I had not been true to some of my core beliefs. For example, being close to my daughter was one of the primary reasons for my leaving my corporate job in Japan. However, by assuming a CEO role in an international venture, I continued to travel often to remain far away from my little girl and from the woman who would become my new wife.

It was during the reflection phase, that I realized how perfect my business failure had really been. The events were a great lesson in humility and they gave me a chance to find alignment with my core beliefs and to have an opportunity to find real success in life.

In hindsight, what would you have done differently?

I am not really sure. Perhaps if I had really understood what true success in life is earlier in my life, I would have made many different decisions. At times, I think that having a coach or a mentor at the time I decided to start my venture would have helped me a great deal. At the same time, it is possible that I would not have taken the chances I took. However, many critical events (such as meeting my wife), would not have taken place either. In my view (and experience), there is a perfection in all events that take place. Being able to understand such perfection, requires a kind of wisdom than most of us are not able to acquire in a lifetime.

What advice would you give people thinking about a career change?

Invest time and energy in getting to know yourself—your values, strengths, weaknesses, and dreams. Understand the importance of seeking and asking for help (this is one lesson I'm still learning). Once you know where you want to go, make a plan and pursue your dreams with gusto. Use your intuition to help you make critical decisions. Learn from your failures and from your enemies. Both can be great instructors if you pay attention.

Do you feel you are in the right career for you at this point in time?

Yes. After experiencing my first significant lesson of failure in business, I realized that our ability to create new things is unlimited. Now, I have two small businesses. Both of them touch the lives of the people we serve and both are profitable and growing. Financially, things are still a bit tight. But overall, I feel I'm on the right path and that the best times are yet to come. In the meantime, I derive an enormous amount of pleasure from spending quality time with my wife and three children. I feel truly blessed and I know that really being in the moment is the only thing I have control over. Nothing else is guaranteed. This realization makes life rich and relevant.

FROM NONPROFIT ADMINISTRATOR TO LIFE COACH

Name: Debbie
Previous career: nonprofit administrator
Years in previous career: 5
New career: life coach
Years in new career: 3
Personal status at time of transition: 31 years old; engaged

Tell me a little about your career as a nonprofit administrator.

My first position at a nonprofit agency was providing counseling and outreach services to youth and their families. After a year I moved out of doing direct service and became a full-time project manager overseeing grants and reports for a few different programs. Two years later I was promoted to department director. My department had a staff of 30 and six supervisors reported to me. I planned and managed budgets, facilitated department meetings, chaired the Diversity Committee, did grant writing, attended several meetings with collaborating partners, and participated as part of the management team at the agency for strategic plans, policy issues, and other agency-wide needs

What caused you to change careers?

After being promoted to an upper-management position, I soon realized that while I was capable of doing the job and proud of having a position like that at a relatively young age, I was not happy. I felt drained, overwhelmed, and completely tapped out of any creative abilities. I didn't feel like myself at work. Although I learned a lot and was grateful for the opportunity to step into a leadership role, I felt depleted.

How did you decide what you wanted to do next?

I remember knowing what I didn't want to do, but not knowing what it was I wanted to do. It wasn't just the job itself, it was the career of social work that I wanted to move away from. So, I allowed myself to think outside the box and consider other things that I might be interested in.

I thought about the elements of my job that I had enjoyed in the past. I really like supervising people and helping them reach toward their goals. I knew I had a talent for bringing out the best in a group and I enjoyed working with groups. All these thoughts were circling around in my head, but I still wasn't sure what to do next.

Right about this time I had the opportunity to work with a coach. She had worked at the same organization I did before becoming a coach and I thought she would be able to help me gain the perspective I needed to decide what to do. As I worked with her, I became intrigued with the possibility of becoming a coach myself.

My coach directed me to a website that described all the different coach training programs, and I began researching those. I read some books on coaching and I talked with other coaches I knew. I also took advantage of the free introductory courses in coaching that some of the coaching schools offer. I found a program that was a great fit for what I was looking for and enrolled that June.

Coaching sparked my creativity for the first time since my undergraduate days. I felt alive again and excited about learning. I knew I had found the right path for me.

How long did the actual transition take from decision to being hired?

Because I had a background in helping professions, I didn't have to start at square one with the coaching program. I was encouraged to start coaching people pro bono to gain experience, so I worked with my first client in August of that year. It was incredibly rewarding and I was on cloud nine. I decided to make a plan to leave my job. I wanted to be gone by December; but it didn't work out that way.

What obstacles or breakdowns did you experience along the way?

Just as I was starting to let certain people at work know about my plans to leave the job, my fiancée, with whom I had lived for 6 years, broke up with me. Not only was that emotionally the hardest thing I had ever gone through up to that point, but the thought of paying for everything on my own sent me into a tailspin.

For the first time, fears came up about whether I could really make this work. I received a great deal of support from my coach training instructor as well as a student in my class. I was able to work through my fears, and I decided that if I waited a little longer, I'd have a little more money saved up. I told myself that if I couldn't make ends meet, I'd just get a job and it wouldn't be the end of the world.

There were also obstacles about the timing of various tasks at work. Some major things were coming up at my job that I really felt I needed to be present for—end-of-year reports, grants due at the beginning of the year, etc. I also had personal goals for things I wanted to accomplish, or at least set in motion, before I left. I had been there for 6 years and although I wasn't happy with my job, I was very connected to the organization's mission and many of the people who worked there. I'm pleased that I was able to accomplish certain goals as I was transitioning out of the job.

What did you learn about yourself as you went through this process?

So much! I learned that I can create anything I set my mind to. Once I had the clear vision, and felt it in my bones, it was as if the universe couldn't move fast enough to bring me exactly what I needed to keep moving forward. Even the difficult relationship breakup was a blessing. Only 6 months later I met a man and fell in love. That, too, did not happen in the timeline I had envisioned. He wasn't supposed to show up for at least another year, but I had to accept the timing because everything else that happened in the right ways for me had come early. This was no exception.

I learned to trust myself deeply and unequivocally. I learned that I am not someone who can settle, even if the income is great and the people at work are supportive. I need more in my work and in my life. I have experienced what it's like to be fully alive, creatively expressing my gifts, and I won't ever go back to the way I was living before.

In hindsight, what would you have done differently?

I was blessed. I really wouldn't change anything, not even the times of not knowing and the dark days of being in-between. Those were all places I needed to be. I learned valuable lessons sitting with fear and facing the unknown. I needed to be stripped down so that the core questions could emerge. Because I never really doubted myself or my vision, the transition came fairly easily. The transition was not hard; the time *before* the transition was the hardest—when I dragged myself to work and felt like crying at the end of everyday. *That* was painful. The transition was a relief and a gift.

What advice would you give people thinking about a career change?

Avail yourself of professional help. It is seriously the best thing you can do. It's too hard to be in your own head churning over a decision. Having a coach or some other professional to guide you in becoming clearer and overcoming your fears is invaluable.

In general, I would say that no change happens until two things grow large enough to outweigh any fears you may have: (1) dissatisfaction with your current situation and (2) excitement about your vision. My favorite quote is by Anaïs Nin: "And the day came when the risk it took to remain tightly closed in a bud was more painful than the risk it took to bloom."

Do you feel you are in the right career for you at this point in time?

Absolutely! All the signs are there that this is the right career for me. I feel lit up when I'm doing my work. There's tremendous satisfaction and happiness to be able to use all parts of me as I help others reach their goals. I feel centered, completely myself, and at home.

Making a change in one area of your life affects all others. Be prepared for your life to change. This doesn't mean it will be bad or hard or even necessarily that huge, but it will be different. Instead of fearing these shifts, embrace them. You set them in motion and you needn't fear the chain reaction. Everything is related and when you set out on a path to improve your life, you must trust what happens along the way.

For Your Reference

Further Reading

Additional WetFeet Resources

About the Author

The books and websites on this resource list will provide you with additional information and inspiration to help you successfully transition to the career of your dreams.

Further Reading

Finding Your Own North Star

(Martha Beck, Three Rivers Press, 2001)
The North Star is a fixed point in the sky that has been a guide to sailors for years. This book skillfully combines information, exercises, and real-life stories to help you find the true direction of your life, or your own North Star.

I Could Do Anything If I Only Knew What It Was

(Barbara Sher, Dell Publishing, 1994)
Do you feel your life has lost its focus? This book will help you recapture long lost goals and overcome the obstacles and roadblocks that are holding your back from reaching your dreams.

The Pathfinder

(Nicholas Lore, Simon & Schuster, 1998)
Nicholas Lore, founder of the Rockport Institute, provides the reader with an in-depth, step-by-step strategy for designing a career that will be both rewarding and fulfilling.

The Power of Purpose: Creating Meaning in Your Life and Work

(Richard J. Leider, Berrett-Koehler Publishers, 1997)
Do you want more from life than just going to work and doing your job? This book provides a practical guide for creating a life filled with passion and meaning.

Second Acts:
Creating the Life You Really Want, Building the Career You Truly Desire

(Stephan Pollan and Mark Levin, HarperCollins, 2003)

You have a second act in life. Make it the best it can be! Combining real-life stories with practical exercises, the authors provide an easy-to-follow road map for your journey to a more satisfying life.

True Work: Doing What You Love & Loving What You Do

(Michael Toms and Justine Toms, Bell Tower Publishing, 1998)

Are you consumed by your work? Has your work lost all meaning and enjoyment for you? It doesn't have to be that way. This book discusses how to transform your view of what you do so that it becomes a source of enjoyment and refreshment instead of just drudgery.

What Would You Do if You Had No Fear?
Living Your Dreams While Quaking in Your Boots

(Diane Conway, Inner Ocean Publishing, 2004)

The author has asked this question of people from all walks of life. This book is a collection of their stories, and it will provide hope and inspiration to anyone who feels that his or her life is held back by the tentacles of fear and uncertainty.

What's Next? Women Redefining Their Dreams in the Prime of Life

(Rena Pederson, Pedigree Books, 2001)

This book explores the lives of successful women—famous and not-so-famous—who have redefined themselves midlife. This is a practical and inspirational book that will empower you to let go of other's expectations, to say no when necessary, and to decide what's next and what's best for you.

The Way of Transition: Embracing Life's Most Difficult Moments

(William Bridges, Perseus Publishing, 2001)

In this powerfully honest book, Bridges takes the reader on the incredible journey of his own transition after his wife of 35 years dies of breast cancer. Bridges skillfully weaves chapters about his own struggle with transition with chapters on his theoretical expertise in transition. The result is a beautiful, poignant, and insightful book that will help and support anyone who has suffered a life change and who has struggled through the trials of a transition.

Additional WetFeet Resources

WETFEET INSIDER GUIDES

The following WetFeet titles are all available online at www.WetFeet.com and www.Amazon.com. See the last 2 pages of this Insider Guide for a complete list of WetFeet Insider Guides.

Ace Your Interview!

Learn what employers are looking for and how to give it to them in an interview, from key preinterview research through interview prep for commonly asked questions and curve balls, through effective follow-up strategies.

Negotiating Your Salary and Perks

This Insider Guide will give you the tools to maximize your salary, title, responsibilities, perks, work flexibility, and more by teaching you how to negotiate the terms of your next job from the moment you start looking for it.

Networking Works!

Find out how you can get the jump on those great jobs you hear about but never seem to see postings for, and what it takes to land them yourself, from the initial contact through all-important lunch meetings and follow-up.

Job Hunting A to Z: Landing the Job You Want

This information-packed guide covers the basics of networking, interviewing, and negotiation all in one handy reference, with tips on drumming up contacts and referrals, handling weird interview situations, and choosing from several offers.

Killer Cover Letters and Resumes!

This guide covers the basics that everyone should follow to write truly effective resumes and cover letters, from evaluating your skills and determining what you have to offer prospective employers to the top five recruiter's pet peeves to avoid to solutions for special cases such as lack of experience or gaps in employment.

WetFeet's Company Profiles and Interviews

Get the lowdown on hundreds of high-profile employers, including key numbers, personnel highlights, key facts, and an overview for each company. www.wetfeet.com/research/companies.asp.

WetFeet's Real People Profiles

Get the inside scoop on different career paths from people who are actually working in them. WetFeet interviewed hundreds of professionals across industries to learn what they do in a typical day, how they got their jobs, what they love and hate about them, and what you need to know to get into a similar job. www.wetfeet.com/research/RPP/RPPlistbyCareer.asp

About the Author

Mary Ann Bailey, MC, is a life coach who specializes in working with people going through career transitions.

Mary Ann's expertise in career transition is a combination of personal and professional experience. She started her career path in the field of education. She taught junior high and high school for 10 years before deciding to change careers. She returned to school and received a master's degree in counseling. On completing her counseling internship, she was hired as a youth and family counselor at a mental health agency. She worked for 4 years doing direct service work and then she was given the opportunity to move into the role of program director. Three years later she was promoted to associate director of the agency.

After working for 12 years in the nonprofit sector, Mary Ann decided it was once again time for a career change. At this point in her life, her priorities had changed. She wanted to do something that was more personally fulfilling, something that combined her strongest skills with her deepest passion, and something that gave her greater flexibility in her work schedule. Coaching seemed like the perfect answer. She started her own coaching business, Bailey & Associates Coaching, and has helped people from all walks of life transition to more personally satisfying and rewarding careers.

Mary Ann holds a BA in psychology, a master's in counseling, and is a graduate of the Integral Coaching Program of New Ventures West in San Francisco. She is a member of the International Coach Federation and the Puget Sound Coaches Association. For more information about Mary Ann, visit her website at www.baileycoaching.com.

WETFEET'S INSIDER GUIDE SERIES

Job Search Guides

Getting Your Ideal Internship

Job Hunting A to Z: Landing the Job You Want

Killer Consulting Resumes!

Killer Cover Letters & Resumes!

Killer Investment Banking Resumes!

Negotiating Your Salary & Perks

Networking Works!

Interview Guides

Ace Your Case: Consulting Interviews

Ace Your Case II: 15 More Consulting Cases

Ace Your Case III: Practice Makes Perfect

Ace Your Case IV: The Latest & Greatest

Ace Your Case V: Return to the Case Interview

Ace Your Case VI: Mastering the Case Interview

Ace Your Interview!

Beat the Street: Investment Banking Interviews

Beat the Street II: I-Banking Interview Practice Guide

Career & Industry Guides

Careers in Accounting

Careers in Advertising & Public Relations

Careers in Asset Management & Retail Brokerage

Careers in Biotech & Pharmaceuticals

Careers in Brand Management

Careers in Consumer Products

Careers in Entertainment & Sports

Careers in Health Care

Careers in Human Resources

Careers in Information Technology

Careers in Investment Banking

Careers in Management Consulting

Careers in Marketing & Market Research

Careers in Nonprofits & Government Agencies

Careers in Real Estate

Careers in Retail

Careers in Sales

Careers in Supply Chain Management

Careers in Venture Capital

Industries & Careers for MBAs

Industries & Careers for Undergrads

Million Dollar Careers

Specialized Consulting Careers: Health Care, Human Resources, and Information Technology

Company Guides

25 Top Consulting Firms

25 Top Financial Services Firms

Accenture

Bain & Company

Booz Allen Hamilton

Boston Consulting Group

Credit Suisse First Boston

Deloitte Consulting

Deutsche Bank

The Goldman Sachs Group

J.P. Morgan Chase & Co.

McKinsey & Company

Merrill Lynch & Co.

Morgan Stanley

UBS AG

WetFeet in the City Guides

Job Hunting in New York City

Job Hunting in San Francisco